The Artist's CURSE

Artists are born.

Artists are made.

CURSE 3–THE AIR YOU BREATHE

Artists create out of a mystic call.
Failure to give your vision form creates a toxic residue in you. **SUFFOCATION**.

Then again, failure to deliver a form is part of the creative process.

Continue breathing.

CURSE 4–THE CORE

At the center of the art world lies the artist. Without artists, there wouldn't be

collectors,
galleries,
museums,
art fairs,
or auction houses.

Unfortunately, many artists feel out of the equation.

Continue creating.

Many artists shy away from exposing the difficulty of sustaining their careers. Instead, they prefer to portray an image of continuous success.

But behind the curtains, artists **scream**, slam doors, and sometimes curse

the

day

they

were

born.

Art schools teach you everything, but not the connection between art and your soul, between art and an art career, **between art and the art market.** Once you understand these relations, you will

free

yourself

to

create

better

art.

Sometimes, the art world looks like a vast industrial farm operating underground without transparency and regulations. You can only guess who is bullying, milking, butchering, or even skinning you alive.

Navigating the art world was never easy and never will be. Your only rescue is to

continue making great art **at any stage in your career.**

In the beginning, all artists create out of passion. And as life goes on, at one point, they realize that their living depends on selling their art. So it is almost inevitable to feel you are selling a part of you, a piece of your soul, suddenly evaluated, priced, split into editions, **bid over,** and traded.

Artists are not for sale. Their artworks are. You often hear collectors, patrons, gallerists, auction houses–even artists–equating an artwork to its creator.

"I have bought a Picasso.
I have sold a Picasso."

PICASSO

**was
never
for sale
but
his
Art
is.**

When an artwork is born,
it will have a life of its own.

To remain focused on the
journey and to avoid
contamination,

divorce yourself from your art.

As an artist,
you are
alone.
But you will
always be part
of a greater
constellation.

Artists soon realize the number of systems entrapping them as they

prog**ress.**

Art is a process of liberation, of dissolving all labels, barriers, and constructions. If you feel that the art world system freezes your progress, affects your psychology, and contaminates your vision, your challenge will be to **remain true to yourself** while being aware that this self and your art are forever changing. Many artists will eventually bend.

Bad art, books, and films exist for a reason.

They lack the artist's original spirit.

Value in the art world is tricky and doesn't follow the logic of banknotes, where numbers determine value. And that's why art can

change all realities.

Art materials like fabric and pigment cost little. But the art system processing these ingredients can push the artwork's price to unimaginable figures to hundreds of millions. Salvator Mundi, one of the ugliest paintings and possibly a fake, went under the hammer at Christie's New York in 2018 for:

"Making money is art. And working is art. And good business is the best art."

Not everyone can be Andy Warhol.

As an artist, you have exceptional assets. Putting your artwork's intrinsic value aside, you can play the game to create any value you imagine for your art. **But is your art about playing games?**

In the art market, the value of canned shit varies and is not dependent

on the artist's diet.

Think of Manzoni's canned shit or *Cloaca*, the poo machine by Wim Delvoye. Some collectors would pay more money for shit from New York than Lahore **or** Guadalajara.

It's natural that collectors are careful what shit they invest in and what kind they hang in their living rooms.

At age eight, my daughter's best friend, Emi, once asked me these questions to understand what art is while comparing her drawings to established artists. She wanted to know why her drawings would be worth 50 cents while those of established artists, which she felt resembled her own, would sell for **$50,000.**

She asked me,

How do you know when you have created a work of art?

When does a work become art?

Who decides it is a work of art?

A poem doesn't need a publisher to validate its verses. It exists once written or recited. And a painting doesn't need a gallery or a museum.

You don't create art because you have to make an exhibition. Create art first and think later about where to exhibit it, just like when you write a book, you don't worry about the publisher but about writing your story.

Focus your energy on what matters.

You decide when your art is done. And from there, its own journey **starts.**

A collector once acquired an artwork I featured on my website without seeing it in reality. When he received the shipment, he called me right away in anxiety, saying,

"I'm looking at both images at the same time, and I'm sorry Steve, but I like the one on the website more."

How could I know what colors he sees on his screen? **Once you declare your artwork is born, it will have a life of its own and an image of its own.** This you cannot control.

Most people will see your art online or reproduced. But this dilemma shows the importance of seeing the original artworks finished and signed in

the artist's way.

"An artist entering an art fair is like a teenager barging into his parent's bedroom while they're **having sex,**" said artist John Baldessari.

In art fairs, you walk for two or three days what feels like hundreds of kilometers, from booth to booth, corridor after corridor, in a **never-ending loop**. Once after Frieze art fair in London, I felt so sick that I said,

"If you ever see me at Frieze again, **spit on me,** but if you ever see my art hanging there, you fucking buy it."

On the first day of my master's degree in Art Business at Sotheby's Institute of Art in London, the lecturer wrote a few words on the board, then **turned around** to recite them slowly so that we understood **what art from an art market perspective is,**

"If it doesn't sell, it's not art."

In the classical understanding of the art market,

provenance,
exhibition history,
critical reception, and
auction house records

are the key factors that determine the artwork's value. Aim to have a dose of each if you wish to increase the value of your art. **But some artists dare** and break all the rules, creating new factors.

They did all the wrong things and **got it right.**

Arrive at your exhibition opening at least two hours in advance. More than once I saw my work hanging **upside down.**

When you think curators or professionals will refer to your website, books, or even the clear hanging marks at the back of the artwork, they won't.

Be clear about the instructions, especially relevant when you exhibit internationally and you only fly to the opening.

This inspired me to create art where its **orientation** does not matter sometimes.

Artists, born or made, always seek **endless recognition.**

Recognition should never be the purpose of your art. Don't wait for recognition or depend on it for any actual relief, no matter its quantity or **quality.**

Some artists find in God a source of energy to fuel their creations. But what if the artist doesn't have a God? Where would the energy then come from? Some artists believe themselves to be the highest Creator. Religious or not, you are bound to discover the most extraordinary power **lies in secret within you.**

When you work on a new series, it is almost inevitable to be impressed by the power of the first two and then struggle to match their force as you continue working. This is because you start thinking of the process and technique instead of letting yourself flow like in the beginning.

Only when you

find the silence **between your thoughts** will you be able to immerse yourself in the colors of your canvas again.

On the other side of every problem lies a solution. Looking at the problem only affirms, confirms, and magnifies its dimension.

Focus on

the solution.

Before you know it, you will have opened

many

windows of possibility.

Art sets you on the route of becoming human, a citizen of planet Earth, and one day even **beyond.**

The story of art is the story of life.

Because life is impossible to get,
we will always be doing art.
The journey of art
is

endless.

Art is a journey of self-interrogation and introspection. A continuous state of transformation. Don't fear death as an artist. **Surrender to a new you**.

Once, when I thought it was all over,
a friend sent me this:

“Just when the caterpillar thought the world was over, it turned into **a butterfly.”**

Going for a walk, you see something inspiring and think the visual and what it triggered will linger within you **forever**. It won't. Then, just as you lie down to sleep, another epiphany hovers above your head, and you let it wait till the morning to write it down. Upon waking, **it's gone.**

Take notes.

All of your ideas, your feelings, and inspirations are like clouds. They keep moving. And before you know it, they shower on **someone else.**

Sometimes, you **have no idea** where your great inspirations come from. When in doubt, read curse 28 and **never carry an umbrella!**

Inspiration is like the air we breathe. You don't see it, but **it's always there.**

Inspirare originally means "to breathe." Early uses of the word also meant "to move or guide through a **divine** or **supernatural** agency or **power**." When you feel uninspired,

take a **deep** breath.

When making art, you create for an audience of **one—you**. Be honest in your creations, as honesty is the artist's sharpest and most authentic tool. Artists who mask their emotions fool their

eyes first.

Lying in my bed one early morning after a night of no sleep, I opened my laptop and read these words on social media posted by an artist during her **trip to Washington, D.C.**

“ I listened to a tour guide at the National Gallery ask his group what made Rothko great. Someone said: ‘The colors are beautiful.’ Someone else mentioned how many books and articles had been written about him. A third person pointed out how much money people had paid for his paintings. **The tour guide said:** Rothko is great because he forced artists who came after him to change how they thought **about painting.”**

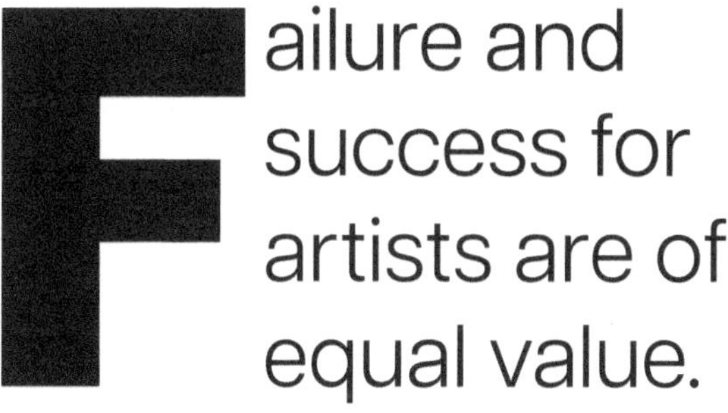

Failure and success for artists are of equal value.

Thomas Edison would have never reached the light without all his failed experiments. Don't let success inspire your ego to forget **the power of failure.**

They often ask artists to write about the essence of their work when applying for grants, residencies, biennials, exhibitions, or commissions.

How would artists know what their art is about before they start their journey with it? There is no point in writing a book if a writer knows how the story develops page by page **until the end.** At one point, it's inevitable that the characters, just like brush strokes, create a reality of their own by **telling their own story.**

Applications kill the artistic progress. The essence emerges only when artists delve into their creations. After that, artists can fill out forms about their creative process.

CURSE 35–THE CURATOR'S GIFT

At least twice curators who exhibited my work have asked me to

gift them an artwork.

I declined to avoid a conflict of interest. It's up to you, but know you risk **never** working with that curator again if you don't do it.

CURSE 36–THE GALLERY OF YOUR DREAMS

It's this easy–the best gallery to represent you is the one you like and whose owners like you back. Create space for synergy, and you are bound to grow together and form a bond **more powerful than a brand.**

I was once on tour to view the archive of tens of thousands of artworks in Tate Modern's museum collection in London. I remember the endless rows and stacks of artworks shelved up to the ceiling in all shapes and forms. The smell of paint, varnish, lacquer, fabric, earth, elephant dung, and other chemicals still lingers in my nose and upsets my stomach. When I asked,

"How often do these artworks see the light of day?"

The cemetery warden answered,

"Almost never."

At that point, I wondered why I was doing art and why many artists pushed to have their works buried in museums.

This taught me to be at **peace** when collectors hang my art in living rooms.

Navigating the art world is like entering

an eternal maze
without an exit.

You will often find success in its chambers, but you are also bound to get lost many times, feel isolated, hitting wall after wall.

Don't despair!

What you might perceive as **dead ends** often hide **secret doors**. Keep working and imagining, and before you know it, you will

see
new
directions.

CURSE 39—WHAT CAME FIRST?

Once, I chatted with a museum curator in Berlin about artists and their role in history. To clarify his point, he said that artists exist because there are museums that exhibit their art.

Cave paintings are now museums because **hairy men** and women drew onto their walls. When in doubt, see curse 4 as a reminder.

CURSE 40—THE MASTER OF LIGHT

The artist's quest should be the creation of unique visuals—to **unveil images never seen before.**

Trust your gut feeling and keep working **until the art shines in your eyes.** Only then will it shine in the eyes of others.

CURSE 41–DECEPTION

I learned that my art and I can never be one. My art, however, will always be a part of me.

An autobiography is only a window into the writer's life–never the entire story. And there can never be a complete story.

CURSE 42–THE UNIVERSE

The history of the world is a history of images. One day we might discover the world itself is nothing more than an image. Since the dawn of time, our quest has been to decode this image. Consequently, we have contributed bits and pieces to solving this great puzzle. When resolved, we are either liberated, or **it's game over.**

CURSE 43–THE OBSESSION

The image of the world and our presence in its reality has **obsessed artists** since time immemorial. Our quest to understand this fixation and liberation from it will always be futile.

CURSE 44–THE PUZZLE OF ALL PUZZLES

There has never been an artwork that looks at life from all perspectives. And there never will be. All artworks are small pieces of a giant puzzle whose beginning and end no one can imagine. And because we can never solve this puzzle,

we will always **make art.**

The thought by philosopher and art historian Georges Didi-Huberman that **changes everything.**

"We need pictures to create history, especially in the age of photography and cinema. But we also need imagination to re-see these images, and thus, to **re-think history.**"

Rarely ask for opinions from others in the process of creation. Listening to different voices might be a recipe for disappointment. Becoming an artist is the journey of finding your inner voice. By listening to it, you will get **the best advice.**

When you feel lost,
close your eyes.

In the darkness, the eyes
begin to see.

Making art involves **deletion**, subtraction, and erasure of digging into essence. **Learn the art of less** to avoid lifeless scenes in films, extra brushstrokes, useless explanations in writing, and redundant words in a poem.

Elimination makes any work of art stand out even though the entire process is one of **addition.**

Don't rotate around your thoughts. When in doubt, throw it out, a cliché that still has power.

CURSE 48—SHUT UP

I transformed my pain into art for many years, only to find it necessary later to free the art from my pain. Don't over-explain your art. Doing so limits it to your categories and labels. Learn **the art of shutting up** so people can create their own stories when they see your art.

CURSE 49—THE ART CAREER

Every career gets its dose of **challenges.** But these challenges will allow you to continually find ways to renew yourself while creating new roots and routes.

In 2007, I chatted with an artist from Tehran during our group exhibition in Istanbul. We spoke about the value of our works, a few thousand dollars back then. A year later, Bonhams auction house opened in Dubai, and for the first time in the region's history, this artist broke the **one million dollar mark,** shifting the course of his career.

In the world of art, everything is **possible.**

CURSE 51–ARTISTS ARE FROM EVERYWHERE & NOWHERE

The world of art
has no beginning
and no end.

CURSE 52–WHICH ONE IS IT?

I once received an invitation to a show that read,

> "We would like to welcome you to the exhibition of the Female, Palestinian, Christian, Artist ... "

If asked, most artists secretly prefer **no labels** whatsoever, including "artist."

CURSE 53–ONE OR TWO

True collectors buy with their eyes and heart, not their ears and pockets. But those are very rare. And you will struggle in your life as an artist to find a score of good collectors. At this stage of my career, I can count the people who acquired my art after falling in love on maybe two hands.

Ok, one.

CURSE 54–THE GUARDIANS

Whether they are aware of it or not, **art collectors are custodians of history.**

Don't work on too many projects at once. Over the years, as projects accumulate and some get **stuck**, you will feel overwhelmed and burnt out. When this happened to me, it was refocusing on completing one major project at a time that helped me get back on track. No writer will write the end of three novels at the same time. You finish them **one by one**.

The text should never fill gaps in visual art–powerful images create their own statements. If you feel something is missing requiring you to explain your art with words on walls, see it as a sign to continue working **on your canvas**.

Great visuals speak on their own. In cinema, scenes tell their stories without needing the film director to stop the screening to explain missing details. There is no second **chance.**

How often do you see people in museums or galleries eager to read the exhibition text before even looking at any artwork? **Skip the queue** and see the art like a butterfly flying from one attraction to the next. The text is only a suggestion, and it will serve you better after you've done your own **reading of the art first.**

To increase the chances for your art to survive the test of time, create images like those in **curse 40**. Any statement I wrote about my art in the past is already irrelevant today. Can you imagine its relevance **one hundred years from now?**

What will remain is the power of the image, not its statement.

Some artists believe they can only work when surrounded by

positive

energy.

Fortunately, time teaches us how to cultivate

negative energy and

transform it into art.

See the life work of David Hockney and how his art mirrors his reality at all stages of his career.

Between void and matter, between negative and positive, **imagine infinite possibilities** for your art.

The Venice Biennale, the world's biggest art event, was built on division, pavilions cut into national sections. However, as spectators, even though we rush to see this or that national pavilion, don't we expect to

see art that transcends
borders?

Art dissolves all nationalities as much as geography dissolves in the world of art.

A great poem, film, or song need not rely on its creator's national identity to surface in the world. Remember the ecstasy of Gangnam Style?

Art has the power to float in **everyone's imagination,** and imagination has no borders.

The work becomes universal when artists realize that while looking at the self, they **see many others.**

So don't wait to be discovered. It's your creativity that grows and spreads everywhere. The journey **starts where you are.**

As artists, we wish our art is most relevant to our time and future.

If true, and we really care, why do we forget most of the exhibited art in no time after attending art fairs or gallery weeks?

Between Kassel and Venice, the two most significant art cities, **how many artists will history remember?**

Art emerges from looking deeper into **the details** of life, which is hard everyday work.

Artists spend their lives learning, refining, taking all the time to improve their skills as they become experts, eventually **masters in their field.**

The
only
way
to
become
a
master
is
to
always
remain
a
student.

As an artist, you are
always becoming.

If you think you are **a master**,
your curiosity is at risk.
To relapse, open your inner door
and let yourself out.

CURSE 65—THE MOST COMPLICATED LETTER I KNOW

imagine

You may see your art as your main source of energy. But when it hits troubled waters, you might get sick. That's why **the divorce** from your art in curse 9 helps.

Art should never be the sole source of energy. Sales, critical acclaim, and great exhibiting spaces can never replenish the reservoirs. What does work is your endless faith in what you do and who you are. And **who you are is forever changing.**

Someone gave me a mug inscribed with the words:

Be Different.

My first reaction was:

Be Yourself.

Only then you stand out.

Perceive life or your art career as a curse and you will mainly see them from this angle. Why bring negative thoughts when what you wish for is **the inverse?**

Constant focus on negative thoughts inevitably makes them **the dominating reality.** And when this is true, feeling your life as bliss leads to transformative **power.**

Thoughts, just like art, spread frequencies. Aim to transmit the best ones.

Art is endless research into the well of self. The deeper you

you are bound to discover that the self is a hole stretching to **infinity**, realizing you are

everything and nothing.

During a solo exhibiting black and white prints, someone rushed to me to express her fascination with one particular artwork, inquiring,

"I love your work, but do you have this one in **color**?"

Identify your weakest skills and improve them. If marketing your art is one of them, learn marketing and negotiation skills through reading, tuning in to online channels, attending workshops, and listening to podcasts. Do whatever works for you.

All artists want is to create art, and for others to do the rest. It's not how it works! For sure, not at the very beginning of your career.

The same applies to design, editing software, or even the language of the city you live in. I have lived in Ber-lin since 2010, and only in 2022 did I start taking the German language seriously. Knowing the language would have created more

possibilities.

Can we really delete an image? Once we press the delete button does the image's presence disintegrate? Where does the deletion go? Does it create empty space? When a human body is buried or burnt, its cells transform into carbon to create **new life**.

An image never disappears. Maybe it only changes form. If we shred or delete pictures, we still possess their mental images which we can rework to create new codes and visuals of particles and pixels. **New art**.

When the art world feels like a circus, the best thing to do is to sit back and watch. **Enjoy**.

Just remember that if you like the show or not, you are also a **player**.

One day you must value your art and put a price on it. For many, it could be during the graduate show. The value set here is critical and will tell if the art was over or underpriced when the exhibition is over.

If the pieces sell too quickly, it's a sign you have under valued your work, and for your next show, increase the value a bit. That's a great place to be. If a few artworks sell or nothing at all, it's a sign that you overvalued your art.

To avoid confusion,
remember curse 8
that you are pricing your art
and not yourself.
Artists are not for sale.

CURSE 76—THE FOUR CIRCLES

Alan Bowness, art historian and art critic, described four circles of recognition through which visual artists pass on their path to fame:

Peer Recognition

Critical Recognition

Patronage by Dealers and Collectors

Public Acclaim

And if this is not overwhelming enough, add a dose of auction house records.

In today's art mess, start wherever you wish, enlightening alternative routes for others.

CURSE 77—THE EXPOSURE

For people to buy your art, they need to see it.

If exhibiting in galleries or museums is hard, consider online platforms. They are improving, incorporating virtual and augmented reality that one day might dominate the viewing experience.

If a gallery sells your artwork for $100,000, deduct:

The 10% – 30% collector discount
Almost every collector wants a special deal.

The 50% gallery commission
Some even request 60% & 70%.

The production costs of 10% – 20%
Depends on the material used and mounting.

The income tax
Depends on where you live.

Based in Germany, I pay 35% income tax on average. But let's lower it to 20% after considering my studio's overall expenses. In brief, for such a deal, my profit would be anything between:

$32,400 – $22,400
Around 25%

Some museums ask for a discount of over 50%. Here, do the calculation alone, and **remember the graveyard of curse 37.**

Some artists consider the 50% gallery commission as lost money. But never forget that galleries pay horrendous rent, publish a catalog, cover art insurance, insane shipments sometimes from fair to fair **across continents,** store your work, network in your name, manage the PR, stock the vernissage and finissage, follow up with collectors and museums, and many other small things that do not cross your mind as expenses – like moral support, phone bills or

headache
pills.

These are responsibilities expected of the gallery. Now your responsibility is to **make great art.**

Increase your collector base by creating art sold at different price ranges set by size, technique, or other factors determining value.

For example, you have a solo show with ten paintings.

If all ten paintings are 2/2 meters and priced at $10,000 each, only people who can pay $10,000 might acquire them.

What if some visitors can afford only $5000 or $1000?

If it works for your art style and concept, create for the same exhibition paintings sized 1/1 meters.

Adding a grid of 20 paintings at 25/25 cm would give depth to your show and increase sales potential. And don't be surprised that you might sell all 25 because they are

affordable!

Some art world practitioners seem to work within the margins of **a fictitious protocol** or manuscript–adhering to its rules. But there is no such thing. In the creative life, the codes and the letters of such a manuscript are printed in the imagination–they can always change.

A flexible and creative approach allows:

artists and galleries,
curators and museums,
collectors and institutions
and the varied combinations
between them to focus on
creativity. And if you still
believe in the bible, such
synergy can create

miracles.

CURSE 82–THE ART MAP

It's always a struggle to maintain creative freedom and vision. And many times, you'll see creatives surrender by submitting to reality or letting go of their careers. **There is always another way,** and the best direction is not the one chartered on a map.

As long as your imagination fuels you, you can create your own routes and **rise above any obstacle.**

CURSE 83–BETWEEN THE VALLEY AND THE MOUNTAIN

Success and failure are two sides of the same coin. Embrace both.

Don't always think of the peak as your final destination.

It's the curve down the valley that offers you the most learning.

From beginners to established artists, creatives should never compromise on how they wish to produce their works. You often see students presenting artworks in smaller sizes or mounted on cheap material for their graduate shows. The common claim is,

"Once I have the money, I'll show it how I really want."

But that day rarely comes if this continues to be your approach. Imagine a film director presenting an unfinished or not properly edited film to a festival, saying,

"Sorry. My budget ran dry. But please, see the bigger picture."

How people see your work for the first time always matters.

CURSE 85—WHERE IS THE LIMIT?

Curators and gallerists can inspire artists to improve the quality of their work. But some make the mistake of telling artists how to do it. Only when artists get lost in the details of their work do they become better positioned to **improve their art.**

CURSE 86—THE CRANE TO THE MOON

There is no end to the ambition of artists and where they wish to reach. We are all fixated on exhibiting on planet Earth, but soon enough, artists will fight for the first **exhibition on Mars.**

CURSE 87—THE SPACE

Exhibit your art in a space that fits the work, not the contract. Don't be tempted to show **in every place.**

CURSE 88—IT'S NOT A SPRINT

Some artists get frustrated because their careers don't move quickly enough. But the artists who run their career like a marathon will end up popping more Champagne **in their life.**

Creating is like going through a storm that can confuse your sense of direction. Be careful when you call your friends asking for advice—they will give it to you with all their heart, but **the best answer is always the one you feel is right.** You are, just like the excellent director of a movie, the only one who has

the bigger picture in mind.

CURSE 90—THE TRUTH

You can lie to anyone, including yourself. However, as you grow as an artist, art will teach you to **be more honest.** You will no longer hide your emotions, thoughts, or being. In the artist's life, hiding is akin to lying. Readers can spot lying writers, just as viewers can feel when artists are not exposing their souls.

We know there can never be an absolute truth. And yet, our mission as creatives is a clear exposure of our **inner truth.**

CURSE 91—YOUR SYMPHONY

If people recognize your work, it's a good sign that you have developed your own voice. The more you express yourself, the clearer your voice **will grow and echo.**

Most books on creativity speak about finding one's voice. But remember that your voice has many pitches. So aim to develop and fine-tune your instrument into a symphony of sounds and visuals—**an orchestra**—conducted by you.

People who don't like your voice can always **switch the channel.**

In art schools, the relationship between students and mentors is essential. But don't fall into the trap of catering your art to the advice of your teachers to get better grades. While guiding you to develop your artistic language, true educators respect **your voice and identity.**

During my first year
in photography school,
I received the best advice
from one of my professors, who said,

"Don't listen to your teachers."

CURSE 93—THE STARTING POINT

All of today's celebrated artists started with the humble sale of their first artwork. If you are a beginner, remember they were in the same position you are in now. The journey of art can be one of the most financially challenging and one of **the most rewarding.**

For people to appreciate your old work, create new art. When all seems lost, creating is your best way forward.

CURSE 94—THE LAZY COUCH

Once the partner of a famous artist nagged at him to do more art instead of lying on the couch, to which he replied,

"I am actually working!"

Continue
dreaming.

Expect nothing to make sense in the art world.

You will find:
auction houses acting like art dealers, and galleries working like auction houses.

You will sometimes find a thin line between curators and critics, collectors and patrons, and before you know it, you might be lost between navigating museums and biennales.

Today, artists think like galleries, collectors, and even auction houses. For example, in 2008, Damien Hirst bypassed the galleries and sold his work through a Sotheby's auction, amounting to a

$198 million

forcing his galleries to be among the bidders. Or so was the story told.

And don't forget the curator's gift of curse 35 when curators become collectors.

Aim for your next project to always be better than the previous one, taking your visual research **forward.**

I once met a writer who had published nineteen books. When I asked him which book he considered the best and which I should read first, he said,

"Clearly, my last one."

Artists are often afraid to open negotiations on a contract with a curator or gallery–what if I lose the opportunity to exhibit my work?

Contracts are written to satisfy and secure all parties involved. So what's the point of binding yourself to an agreement you are not happy with?

Mental contracts, engraved with trust and transparency, are the ones I work with the most. When done with the right people, they save paper. But, if written agreements bring you peace of mind, definitely seek them. A few times, they **saved my ass.**

Never underestimate students or young people who approach you with an idea, an interview, or an opportunity. The least you owe them is to listen and decline gently if you see it not fitting.

Don’t be surprised if these novices assume some of the highest positions in the future. They are also on their own journeys **in the art world**.

When I read this quote by the Dalai Lama, it struck a chord on missed opportunities in the art world:

"Remember that not getting what you want is sometimes a wonderful stroke of **luck.**"

The Artist's need to sell art to earn a living.

CURSE 101—THE FREEDOM

Aim to have an external income **unrelated to art sales** to live a better creative life.

Figure out how to diversify and expand your income so that you can **focus on your art.** Today, it is easy to create an app, open an online business, or offer your expertise as an online course like on Udemy.

Work smarter, not harder.

CURSE 102—THE ARTIST'S FEE

Should you get invited to give talks, or participate in panels or Zoom conferences, don't be shy to inquire gently. This also applies to radio and television. There is usually a budget set aside, and if you don't claim it, they give it to someone else, someone who is **more professional than you.**

The norm is to offer an honorarium.

Failure to include the artist's fee in a project funding plan might disqualify your application, a sign you are not professional enough and don't know what you are getting yourself into. Do you prefer to inquire or end up on the phone calling family and friends to help you pay the house rent?

CURSE 103–THE ART ASSET

Unlike stocks, **the value of art can never drop to zero** and simply vanish. If you collect art, you will still find your stunning painting hanging in your bedroom before falling asleep and after waking up. Putting art market forces aside, the power of art lies in its mystery, an intrinsic value that can soar skyward at any moment.

Don't fight what's out there. **Create** what's not there.

This is how everything original starts.

CURSE 105–THE SHAME

Never copy from other artists. If you find yourself inspired by what others are doing, take their visuals and add new layers to them, new meanings. **A new vision.**

CURSE 106–THE GREATEST ARTIST

Before the invasion of technology, hiding inspiration, copying, and plagiarizing was easy. Artists traveled to other countries, and when they returned to their studios, they copied. They widely quoted Pablo Picasso saying,

"Good artists borrow. Great artists steal."

Don't listen to Picasso.

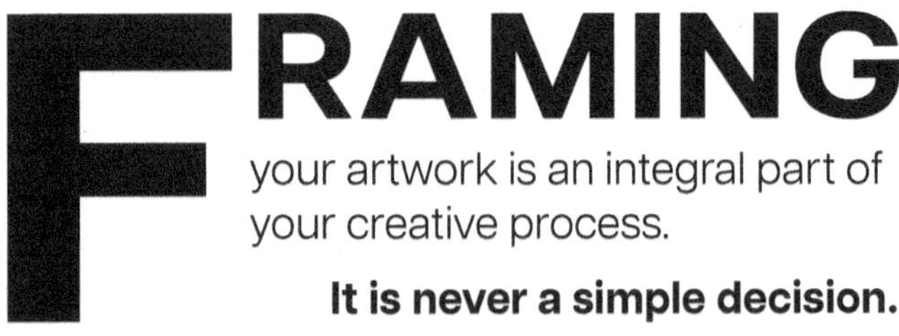

FRAMING

your artwork is an integral part of your creative process.

It is never a simple decision.

When it's right, it boosts the

aura of your work.

And when it does not sit, you will feel it, and so will others.

Don't compromise how you envision your work's display regardless of the pressure exerted by the curator, the gallery, or even the collector. It's your artwork, your responsibility, **your vision.**

See curse 16 on the artwork's image and remember why you sign your artworks.

CURSE 108–THE MISSING SHOTS

Photograph your exhibited art and do it professionally. Installation shots help people grasp your art's actual size and style better. Notice how successful galleries promote their exhibitions.

Installation shots will make a great impression when shared on your website and social media, when sent to anyone interested in your art, or when they get printed in art books.

CURSE 109–OUT OF FOCUS

Unless it's beyond the depth of field, in the world of photography, don't torture the viewer with fuzzy images unless you intend to make

out-of-**focus** artworks.

When you plan it, it is art. Otherwise, use a tripod, improve your focus techniques, and work with **sharp lenses.**

One of your concerns as an artist is how you **authenticate your art,** which you should decide early on. Your signature alone is no longer enough. When I changed my certificates of authenticity after fifteen years of selling my art to serialized QR codes, I had to fly to many countries to adjust them. It cost a fortune.

Today, there is a program that scans the artwork's microstructure to create a unique digital fingerprint for doubtless verification. It's like each artwork has its own digital

Research what works for you and stay on top of your authentication process by remaining consistent. It will save you and your heirs a headache, and collectors and galleries will appreciate **your consistency.**

Initially, **the artist's proof** was a test print of the last run to print the original. Today, it serves as a reward for artists, which they can sell after all artworks sold in the edition. For example, I create my art in an **edition of 6 + 2 APs.**

The value of your art may increase from one edition to the next, and by the time you sell all editions, the artist's proof becomes the most valuable. It's best to keep these proofs for future museum acquisitions or sell them when needed. I see them as

Many artists continue working to the last breath, and there are some schemes in the art world to keep your finances standing in old age. But many artists find these plans risky or never enough.

Your best pension fund is your art. When you keep doing exceptional work, your chance of finding security in your elderly years increases.

CURSE 113–THE MURKY WATERS

The historic art dealer and speculator William Buchanan said in 1824,

"In troubled waters,
we catch the most fish."

Don't trap yourself, and always
remember that it's your art
being caught, **not your soul.**

Collectors and gallerists should never fear artists caught in a storm. Such tornados shuffle the tides creating opportunities that can change the artist's, the collector's, and the gallerist's lives.

CURSE 114–THE GOSSIP

There are no secrets in the art world.
If you don't want it out, don't spit it out.
Today, the air, the room, and of course
your phone have ears.

The monograph, a study on your art, is an invitation into the artist's world. **Artists can navigate their viewers best from one station to another, from one process to the next.** They see the invisible threads connecting the artworks to reveal their vision.

Designers should always consider the artist's way. But don't think you don't need a designer.

They can
do magic.

Collectors shouldn't hesitate to ask artists which one of their works will have the highest market value and potential if they want to know.

Seeing the bigger picture of their careers, the artist's advice is worth much more than many art market professionals.

So if you become a collector, save the fees and commissions and build a real connection with artists. But in return, remember to reward the artist with a sale. **Or two.**

Artists dare.

Courage for artists is like an astronaut's spacesuit. Without it, they will suffocate and die.

For artists who

don't dare,

fear is their number one enemy. Without **fear,** they could reach outer space.

CURSE 119–THE BEGINNING AND THE END

During any creation everything can change, including the beginning, the end and everything in betw**ee**n.

CURSE 120–THE SAVIOUR

And it's not Jesus Christ! You know your life better than anyone else. Learn this early on: **the only one who can really help you**

is 

You would assume that art shippers care about your art the most. Once, a shipper arrived early at my studio **on a rainy day** and informed me hours later via text message that he had left the big crate in front of the house **on the sidewalk.**

Find an art shipper early on in your career that you can trust to deliver the art and process the customs papers properly.

Worrying about exports is one thing, but at one point, you will get dizzy with the mess of importing the art back to your studio.

You will inevitably get tax-audited once, and then they will match every invoice with every artwork to see if it has left the country and returned legally. In other words, if you are not on top of it **now, you are fucked.**

We travel distances to attend expert panels to learn and be inspired, but how often have we felt stuck on auditorium chairs, cursing the day we registered for a worthless conference? Many participants come unprepared, tired, without motivation, speaking without direction.

No, thank you.

Being invited to a panel is an opportunity to share your creativity and expertise. Double-check that your audio, video, and presentation are all functioning.

Wonder why some panels inspired you and

why not.

CURSE 123—NERVES OF STEEL

Given your frequent **journeys into the unknown,** you may sometimes feel you are standing on the edge. Being an artist is like walking on a tightrope, swinging **left** and **right,** directed by sudden forces beyond your control.

To survive, maintain your focus.

Otherwise, you could be thrown off, falling into deeper layers of the unknown.

But once there, remember curse 27, forever a butterfly, and when you feel ready, you will

Once a known patron in the art world visited my studio after attending two art fairs in Berlin and other artist studios. Minutes after leaving, his manager called me and asked if I would like to join them for dinner that evening. At the restaurant, a long seating arrangement waited for us. My name was next to the patron in the middle. When I asked why they seated me in the middle, the manager said,

“My boss told me he liked you and your work the most from all the art he has seen.”

Never underestimate the studio visit. Imagine its floor covered with Aladdin’s carpet. When your guests step on, nobody knows where it could take you. Or, more likely, where the carpet

Artists

who become

mothers

struggle to participate in international exhibitions and art panels, let alone continue their life as artists. Easy access to a fund that offers to pay for **a ticket and a babysitter** must become accessible and the norm.

If you don't commit to your work, no gallery, collector, or art institution will commit to working with you. Their greatest fear is investing in artists who will later

STOP

making

ART.

That's why you often hear questions about your vision, ambitions, and future projects when they first meet you. They want to feel that you were **born to be an artist.**

Auction records created the illusion that artists are born with spoons of **gold.** The spoons are not even **bronze.** But you get shiny moments, and if lucky enough, you will surpass gold with

diamonds.

Like everyone else, artists have to pay rent on time. I've had collectors who paid me a year later and galleries who forgot to notify me they even **sold** my art.

Instead of thinking of **all the reasons** why your next art project, exhibition, or exceptional idea won't work, think of all the reasons why **they will.** This is how you move forward, granting you more chances to reach your ambitions.

Don't focus on the problem
as curse 24 shows you.

Focus on the solution.

Institutions that don't match the energy of the new generation of artists might find themselves buried in the pages of time. See curse 86 with the artist's crane to the moon.

As creatives look beyond space to manifest their visions, institutions must look beyond their concrete walls to remain alive and relevant. But as an artist you always inspire change.

The first rule of life:

adjust,

adapt,

or

die.

Strolling through a bazaar, I checked out a vendor selling ultra-sharp handmade knives. Their high price intrigued me to ask if they ever got dull. He answered,

"All knives require sharpening over time."

As an artist, keep your eyes sharp.
Eliminate visual clutter by looking
into the details of the details.
To see what others don't requires
razor-sharp eyes.

CURSE 131–THE BEAUTY

Every light particle falling on Earth is new. And since **we are creatures of light,** this means we are constantly changing.

CURSE 132–BREAKING FREE

You are the one limiting your energy flow, your creativity, your passion, and your progress. Not the system. You.

CURSE 133–THE BEST EDUCATION

The university of life.

CURSE 134–THE SECRET LIBRARY

When it calls you, pay attention to the

magical library of the **UNIVERSE**

When traveling and exchanging ideas, the books people recommend to you will sharpen your knowledge. Those are the ones you borrow or buy. They are **free** from search engine algorithms, and chances are high you will enjoy them.

Don't seek your Master's degree straight after finishing your bachelor's. It won't be as **rewarding.** You miss out on drawing from real-life experiences to better understand the relationship between theory and practice.

Once during an exhibition, someone approached me asking about one of my artworks, wondering which gallery represented me. The **savvy-looking man** gave me his card, expecting an excellent offer, especially after saying the gallery could google his name.

I got excited. But the gallery sent an invoice 40% higher than my work's actual price, offering a 25% collector's discount upon confirmation of a sale. So practically, the collector would pay 15% more than the fixed price.

The art world is tiny, and collectors quickly feel it when they are being played. Price transparency is critical. That's why today, artists are no longer shy from displaying the value of their art on chosen online art and e-commerce platforms.

Because of this shady game, I left the gallery and lost one of the most prominent photography collectors

in the art world.

In
the
world
of
art,

there is
no reality,

only imagination●

Looking for a particular gallery in Warsaw, I finally found it in an **abandoned** area surrounded by a fence near a series of garbage containers. It was closed on that day, but there was a sign on the door that read,

We participate in **Art Basel.**

A sign not to judge by location but by achievement.

Given the meteoric rise of art fairs in the last twenty years, central locations are no longer seen as the key factor to a gallery's success. Collectors prefer the **glitz and glam** of an art fair. If a gallery contacts you, check their art fair records. A gallery that gets accepted in Art Basel or Frieze is more established than galleries going year after year to satellite fairs like Volta or CONTEXT Art Miami.

On an art panel, an artist was struck by a question from a curator, who asked for his thoughts on his art in relation to **Deleuzian** theory. The artist had no idea what she was talking about, feeling **lost** in **space.**

When someone challenges your knowledge in public, the best way to continue is to speak about your art and practice in relation to your life–the source of all theory. The audience will love to hear you speak from the heart when curators are focused on their mind.

My daughter Cécile came to my studio asking for a new pair of boots. On that gloomy Saturday, I told her,

"Let's wait until Monday and see what happens. We cannot afford it now."

Frustrated, she replied with a grim voice,

"Well, Daddy, what can happen by Monday?"

I said to her,

"The entire universe can flip upside down. The stars can turn off. We can enter a parallel reality. Sometimes, life changes in the blink of an eye."

In my art career, I have seen my universe change from morning to noon, and again by night.

Remember curse 50, **Just Like Magic.** In the world of art, everything is possible.

And yes, Cécile got her boots on Monday!

Some people call art teachers

“failed artists.”

Unfortunately, teaching artists have less time to create art, and many could eventually disappear from the art world's consciousness. But in their hearts, they are artists first.

Once, in an intense debate with a teacher being an artist herself, I expressed that academia leads to the artist's death and that maybe artists shouldn't commit to teaching. Her reply made me change my mind, **thanking every artist-teacher out there.**

“Imagine the state of art schools without artists to guide students. Imagine the dry education they would receive. I would say it's the other way around. Thank God some artists sacrifice their vision to enlighten others.”

On my way to a major art fair in Paris, traffic was crazy, and the queue to the door was going in circles. I took my partner's hand and walked under the rain straight to the front door to be stopped and told that I was at the wrong entrance. After finding the right door, wet, we rushed to the booth and saw visitors taking photos in front of my artworks. But I couldn't believe the gallery I worked with **hung all my art upside down.**

I rushed over to the gallerist to get a pair of gloves, saying that if anyone asked, he should say,

"This is what the artist wanted: to hang his work upside down and then turn it again in public."

Remember curse 20, and show up early to avoid

a public heart attack●

When bored and drained by looking at life from where you are, a change of air helps. Leave your city, country, or even the continent if you can. And if your case is extreme, you could even get lucky enough to leave the planet one day.

In essence,
art is life,
and life is never
dull.

However, a new environment can reset your eyes. But when you **read curse 324**, you

might change your mind.

Per diem or a daily allowance, is sometimes given to artists taking part in international exhibitions. In one show, I noticed how the curator handed over the money daily, bit by bit, drawn out from a wallet or a pants pocket, making some artists feel uneasy.

One evening, I saw two artists take a **can of tuna** from a suitcase in their hotel room. When I asked them why they were not joining us for dinner in a restaurant, they said their mothers had pre-packed meals for them, knowing how expensive Italy is.

On arrival,
exhibition organizers should
hand over all the agreed
amounts in full,
sealed in a nice envelope,
and addressed to each artist.

I never see my time spent doing art as work but as a liberation from work, and that's why I can sit

1000 hours

on one collage.

Many artists see art fairs as **an opportunity to introduce their work to gallerists.** It might work, but the last thing a gallerist wants to explore in those few days is new art. Instead, their attention is on selling the pieces hanging on their booth walls. They are stressed, tired, confused, over-caffeinated, possibly hungover. Always thinking.

Even if you give the gallerist the best quality monograph, chances are, when they tidy up the booth, they will throw your dream book in the garbage bin. **And if you're lucky, the garbage collector will find it and put it on his shelf.**

What works better is establishing contact first and sending the galleries the book by post later, hopefully getting their **undivided attention.**

During art fairs, the talks and chance meetings you have at a bar, on the dance floor, at the after-party, or anytime you **enjoy yourself** are more decisive than any booth visit. This is when the actual business happens.

Many visual artists don't know there is an apparatus out there collecting information and rating artistic activities, quantifying data, giving points or taking them away, ranking artists like stock commodities to reveal their critical worth. As of Sept. 17, 2022, on Artfacts.net, **#1 is Andy Warhol. #5 is Cindy Sherman**. #10 is Thomas Ruff. #100 is Günther Uecker. And the list goes up to hundreds of thousands.

Exhibition history, collections, and gallery representations are the key factors that determine your rating. If you participate in a major biennial like Documenta or the Venice Biennial, your rating will jump a few thousand overnight. An exhibition in New York at MoMA will have much more credit than a museum in Moscow, and clearly, a solo is worth more than a group show.

A collector once advised me to monitor my rating, to which I replied,

"The only thing I should keep an eye on is my **art.**"

But given that the art world believes in numbers, I perform Artfacts maintenance sometimes. They will not list all of your exhibitions quickly unless you pay a subscription. Otherwise, the requested updates will take a few months.

You never know who's watching and what

F**ACT**S

they base their decisions on to work with you or buy your art.

CURSE 149–THE CARE

Take care of your collectors & sponsors. They will be with you, hopefully, for a lifetime. If issues arise, aim always to work it out. Ask them how they are from time to time. They also have hardships. Many will be happy to hear from you, and some might get enticed to work with you **again.**

According to the

greater fool theory

in auction houses, you could be the fool bidding on an overpriced artwork, one you may not even like, acquired for investment, during auction house frenzy, or **God knows** for what. Later, your job will be to find the next greater fool, one who rewards **your foolishness.**

In the world of auctions,
many fools are playing the game.

One day, you might get lucky to have your work labeled blue-chip art, meaning your art sells and resells and is safe for investments, especially after it **hits auction house records.**

There are many ways to increase your art's value–see the four circles of recognition in curse 76 and the poker game of curse 12. But do know, the road to blue-chip reality can make you very di**zz**y.

And when **you become rich,** focus on your art, **not your money.**

If you are looking to **invest in art,** consider not only blue-chip art. Your best bet might be to pay a visit to artist graduate shows or exhibitions of artists at the beginning of their careers. If you have critical eyes, spot the influential artists of the future. By collecting their art at a low price, you support their careers and **inject them with momentum.**

If your instincts were correct, you would enjoy substantial rewards a few years later. And if you're patient enough, one day, you will laugh all the way to the bank, remembering the moment you acquired that small artwork from that young artist on that unforgettable, **exceptional night.**

Once on **a road trip** through the cold mountains of Italy and France, my phone peeped. I had a missed call from a curator. When I returned the call after the holiday, I found out that she was inviting me to exhibit at the Venice Biennale, but given the time I took to call back, she chose another artist.

Since then, I've learned to always get back to anyone looking for me, whether I am at the peak of a mountain or down

in the valley.

Moral Rights—or Droits Morals—are legal entitlements enforced in many countries and designed to protect the creative output of artists, their claim to their work, and how their art is presented.

There are many rights, but let's start with the **"Right of Integrity"** which prevents anyone from modifying or interfering with the artwork. It bans intentional distortion or modifications of a work if that intervention is likely to harm the artist's reputation.

A collector surprised me once by **leading me into the bedroom** to show me how Euphoria got a new frame. It no longer looked like my work. I explained to the collector, who had never heard of moral rights that this was illegal as the change was not confirmed with me and allowed to be seen in public without my permission.

Unlike copyright, moral rights cannot be transferred or assigned to someone else during the artist's lifetime but can be applied after death by beneficiaries and personal representatives.

Also known as the

Right of Paternity.

It allows artists and their estates to **claim ownership of an artwork or to disclaim it.** This is essential when you encounter forged art. If it happens, you have the absolute right to detach your name publicly from it and remove your attribution, warning buyers about its authenticity.

How often do we hear **nagging voices** in our heads as we create, questioning if certain people will like what we do?

Silence these voices. They are useless, at least for now. But when you review and edit your work, call these voices back and listen to their symphony—as long as you remain aware that you are the conductor. Otherwise, your creation might feel contrived, catering to everyone, or at least trying to.

You will be amused at how often journalists incorrectly render the details of your life and art. Always double-check the facts. As for the content, it's none of your business. **It's their view, their vision.**

I don't speak German, so I often ask my partner to go through German reviews. When I gave her a review of my memoir, she scanned every line for an error, and for once, we clinked glasses. But she missed the title, which was brought to my attention after an email inquiry about **The Parachute Complex.**

Learn early on to **document all your art:** its form, **size,** year, technique, exhibitions, bibliography, provenance, and all other details you deem necessary. You will find this information essential for your next art book or monograph. As your career grows and your market expands, the order will save you the headache of looking back in time, searching hard drives, trying to put the pieces of the puzzle of **who, where, when, and what not!**

The ambiguity or lack of enough information on your art history might give speculators room to create fake history, forge your art, and screw you during your life and for sure after your death. And they might get away with it because they have somehow invented a great story to tell the world.

You don't want those you leave behind to curse you for the lack of **order.**

Finding an agent is tricky, and often they are the ones who find you when they spot potential. Meeting them at art fairs is your best bet.

Art agents are well-informed, observe contemporary trends, and have **connections** to private and public collections. They lead people to trust their taste and expertise in shipment, insurance, PR, and other art logistics.

They are **a secret force** in the art world, a special regiment that is hard to reach and classify. They often mask themselves with other labels, like art consultants, advisors, dealers, mediators, and other titles. But when you land on a competent agent, they **could change your entire career.**

I was one of the commissioned artists for the inaugural exhibition of MATHAF: Arab Museum of Modern Art in Doha.

Those were ten days of life at W Hotel, **à la carte** breakfast, lunch and dinner, and a personal driver in a Jaguar. I hardly spent my per diem. And just before the ride to the airport, the commissioner gave a brand new MacBook Air to each of the 23 invited artists. And just a few months later, the museum acquired my work for their permanent collection.

I once showed my work at an exhibition in central London in a building that housed an embassy. The logistics required anyone attending the show to pass strict security clearance. I was held up twice, and I don't think anyone saw that exhibition, not even the security personnel. The curator did not even give artists the per diem promised to them

CURSE 161—AND SO THERE WAS LIGHT

To see the invisible penetrate deeply into the visible.

CURSE 162—THE TIME

No one plays the piano from the first stroke. Instead, creatives learn by giving themselves the time to learn from scratch. **This is how skill and talent develop.**

If people freed their time to focus on their passion, the world would become a more creative space. And by default, a better place.

And **bigger** is not necessarily **better.**

Your art may not be selling because of two factors—**its price and its size.** Large sizes often make for more expensive work. Reducing the price will hit its value in the art market, creating less confidence in your art. Some artists who do so will find it challenging to get back on their feet. If your sales are stagnant, one way is to make new artworks in smaller sizes and price them lower. This will maintain **the value of your old work** while attracting new buyers.

Don't hire interns to make **tea** and **coffee**, to be used and abused. Unfortunately, many are not remunerated for their sincere efforts, dedication, and even transportation costs. A symbolic payment will add to your reputation and give interns more motivation. And who knows, your next intern might become your studio manager.

If you seek an internship, don't do it for your resume, but to learn something new and to get inspired.

This is a right granted to artists or their heirs in some countries to receive a fee on the resale of their art. Applicable during the artist's lifetime or for 70 years **after** their **death.**

Yet many galleries, collectors, and auction houses despise this moral right because it adds to the artwork's price. It was initially intended to champion the cause of the starving artist, rewarding them or their descendants later as their work gained reputation and became more valuable.

Portion of the sale price	Royalties
From 0 to €50,000	4%
From €50,000.01 to €200,000	3%
From €200,000.01 to €350,000.	1%
From €350,000.01 to €500,000.	0.5%
Exceeding €500,000	0.25%

The maximum you can receive is capped at **€12,500,** reached by works sold for €2 million or more.

Only a collecting society like the Design and Artists' Copyright Society (DACS) may collect the royalties.

True patrons find a tacit way to make sure the artists they support have bread on the table in challenging times.

But also, don't burden your patrons every Monday and Thursday with your life.

You

will

risk

losing

them.

CURSE 167–THE EXCUSES

In a moment of inspiration, **does a painter need a brush to paint?** Does a photographer need a camera to create an image? Does a poet need a pen?

Real artists will resort to anything in their hands to execute their art.

The tools are only there to mediate the expression. **The creation is already in you.**

CURSE 168–THE ACADEMY OF ARTS

In your lifetime, you might only get the chance **once**, maybe **twice**, to choose an art university. So make sure you make the right choice. On the Master's level, and for sure for your Ph.D., it makes a difference who your course professors are. Look at their work and see if they fit your direction.

In any case, never forget where you **get your best education**, as curse 133 reveals.

Don't fall into believing that you need a fixed hour or specific space for something to start. For many years, when people asked me:

"Can I visit you in your studio?"

I always replied,

"You just stepped in."

As an artist, you carry your studio with you. Never let a physical place, or lack of it, paralyze your workflow. Your studio is in every step you take, wherever you are. That's why your creation never stops.

I worked from home for almost twenty years until my artworks got bigger, and I needed a place to store them. Luckily enough, I rented the flat opposite mine. I take three steps to enter the studio and only a few minutes to

dissolve into my universe.

If you are determined, the ideal space will find you.

Once a gallery represents you, many people see it as a sign of approval of your art. Depending on which stage in your career, galleries may ask to represent you globally, regionally, or in selected countries. Represented exclusively means that for every sale you make, even if it comes directly to you, you share it:

50/50

in general.

Good galleries have a decent following, are well-connected to museums, collectors, curators, critics, the media, and can push your career forward in many countries.

It's also possible to be represented by several galleries if there is no conflict of interest. For example, it makes geographical sense if you work with a gallery in New York, London, and Seoul. The gallerists will be happy that you have a vast network. But never forget that **what represents you best is the quality of your art.**

Your gallery is not your personal bank. Many are, in fact, struggling. But if necessary, you can always ask your gallery to help you with a down payment, a loan, or guide you towards finding a solution.

The most successful collaborations are when galleries and artists are **transparent** and **trustworthy.** In this relationship, which many describe as a **marriage,** these traits are more valuable than the art assets.

Don't jump to other galleries without agreement with the galleries representing you. Today, artists have multiple professional relationships with several partners in different countries and continents. The ease of travel, finance, and art shipment has allowed for dynamic connections. However, artists and galleries should ride similar wavelengths for this to work. Otherwise, sudden jumps could be seen as betrayals. And let's face it, **nobody likes to feel hurt, or abandoned.**

End it
with grace
and dignity.

Bad solos echo for many years.

People remember.

How often in life do we hardly remember the best meals and never forget the ones that poisoned us? I often feel sick after visiting a terrible exhibition for at least three days. Okay, a week.

A solo is a window into your life; if you don't do it well,
it haunts you.

This was one of the questions I asked the ten candidates for the position of my studio manager:

“Imagine you won a million dollars. What would you do with your life?

I **disqualified** the candidates who answered with schemes of investment or purchase. I continued to consider those whose responses focused on their passion because it tells me if they follow their heart.

But as a joke, I left the decision up to my cat. If **grumpy Tabby** sat on their laps and remained, I told the applicants they had a better chance. In the end, Tabby sat on the lap of one person only, a poet, and it turned out to be the best decision for the studio. And believe it or not, he even had a stepbrother with my family name.

CURSE 175—THE JOKE

One candidate for the studio manager position emailed us a day later. She stated that the selection process wasn't fair, as the **ultimate cat test** caught her by surprise.

CURSE 176—THE EQUATION

If you want your assistants to care about your art, vision, and life, **care** about theirs. This is how you ensure they continue working with all their

If you believe the quality of your art alone will get you into biennales, public and private collections, **think twice.** But your **network** will.

Many artists dread networking. Without getting to know people in person, you might not reach so far in the mainstream art world. If you have a phobia of networking, find agents and assistants to help your art surface **faster.**

But know, you are your best agent.

Take the time to sharpen your skills, remembering the mastership of curse 62 and the reward of the missing skills in curse 72.

There were times when I struggled in my career to balance my sheets to

ZERO.

However, exploiting credit and overdraft has allowed my studio to grow exponentially, as well as crash a few times. Never doubt though, once you reach zero,

zero
is
an
excellent
place
to **start.**

If you find yourself unable to **pay your bank loans,** ask your bank to bundle all your debt to pay it over many years, like in a house mortgage. This way, you won't crash. Of course, the bank will add interest fees, but it doesn't matter. The idea is to stay afloat. After you invested in a solo show that didn't go well, would you prefer to suddenly pay your bank $20,000 or $200 a month until you find ways to **recover?**

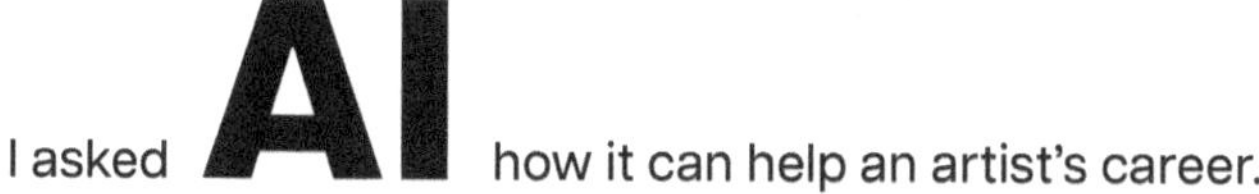
I asked **AI** how it can help an artist's career.

AI can help artists in almost every possible way.

But AI is not the artist.

It does not carry the wound, the obsession, the memory, or the necessity behind the work. It can open doors in the mind, but it cannot decide which door is yours.

Use AI as an assistant, not as a substitute.

Let it expand your field of vision, challenge your habits, and save you endless hours, so you can finally focus on what

matters.

CURSE 181—THE ARTIST PROMOTIONS ON THE TABLE

At your art fair booth, don't underestimate the power of designed handouts, publications, and any other surprise material that could **entice spectators** to dig deeper into the visuals on the walls. Ask the gallery to print hundreds or even invest in some yourself. And don't be astonished when you run out of copies **two days before closing.**

CURSE 182—THE TOXIC IDEA

If you don't transform your inspiring ideas into art as soon as you can, then chances are they **will poison you.** Manifesting them is the greatest relief, and having them linger in the pages of your mind can lead to incredible **pain.**

But even if you reach this great pain, transform the pain into art.

You never know
when the spark
will hit you, but
when it does,
capture the light
and **the ashes** left
behind.

Everything is material for art,
including the artist's shit of curse 13.

It is what it is.
And **it** can be whatever it wants to **BE.**

All words,
negative or positive,
create reality.

Words come from thoughts. If you keep thinking things never work for you, chances are high that they won't.

Listen to Rumi,

"As you start walking on the way, the way appears."

Believe in "the why not" attitude of curse 128 and in the revelation of **what you seek, seeks you** in curse 318. Only then will the universe help **your words create your world.**

A concerned friend asked me not to post art photos online for fear people will use them. I answered,

> The image of art has always been free and will always be. But, there is a price on my artworks because I also transform them into a physical form in a limited edition that people can acquire. Signed.

You want people to **circulate the images of your art.** That's the whole point, and that's how you increase your audience to reach new curators, galleries, and collectors. The last thing you do is add a copyright sign on the image itself. It's distracting and takes away from your artwork's beauty.

I was stuck once in a stinky toilet at **Club Der Visionaire** in Berlin. For minutes, the damn twisted aluminum door wouldn't slide. I tried with force and without, suffocating from taking deep breaths in that stinky toilet. When it finally opened, a man with wild hair asked me what had happened. I said,

The door was **stuck.**

He continued,

Was it you who closed the door?

I said,

No, my father! Clearly, it was me.

Chilled as if he had just landed on a beach in Mexico, he said,

Then why are you angry? Was it you who locked the door?

I realized I was having a mystical experience in the toilet, especially after he said,

Next time, simply don't lock the door. And if you do, don't panic. Remember that you can always open it again.

His statement made me think of all the doors I might have unconsciously closed over the years and inspired me from that moment onwards to keep every door and window in my imagination wide

open!

On Creating & Creation

On Being An Artist

On Navigating The Self

On The Art Market

On Inspiration & Getting Inspired

On Developing Artistic & Mental Skills

On Purpose & Essence

On Imagination

On Validation & Recognition

On Copyright & Legalities

On The Art Career

On The History of Art

On Organization

On The Artist Studio

On Networking

On The Artist's Block

On & Towards Artistic Freedom

On The Artist's Ego

On & Towards Mastership

Steve Sabella is among the rare artists who have lived the art world from both sides: inside the studio, where the work is born, and inside the market, where its value is framed, negotiated, and tested. Born in Jerusalem in 1975 and based in Berlin since 2010, he works across photography, collage, installation, and text, treating the image not as a record of reality but as a force to be reopened: a site of excavation, liberation, and **decolonized imagination.**

His work is held in major public and private collections, including the **British Museum**, London; Mathaf: Arab Museum of Modern Art, Doha, where he was one of twenty-three artists commissioned for the museum's inaugural exhibition; the Institut du Monde Arabe, Paris; the Bahrain National Museum; the Dalloul Art Foundation, Beirut; the Barjeel Art Foundation, Sharjah; Contemporary Art Platform, Kuwait; and the Ars Aevi Museum, Sarajevo.

His work has been presented internationally, including at Les Rencontres d'Arles, FotoFest Houston, the British Museum, Time Space Existence in Venice during the Architecture Biennale, and the International Center for Photography Scavi Scaligeri in Verona, which presented his 2014 retrospective **Archaeology of the Future**.

In 2008, Sabella received the Ellen Auerbach Award from the Akademie der Künste, Berlin, which later co-published his monograph Steve Sabella: Photography 1997–2014 with Hatje Cantz. The book includes texts by Hubertus von Amelunxen and a foreword by Kamal Boullata, who described Sabella's work as "**a dream to discover**."

Sabella holds an MA in Art Business from Sotheby's Institute of Art, London, and an MA in Photographic Studies from the University of Westminster, where he studied as a Chevening Scholar. His memoir, **The Parachute Paradox: Decolonizing the Imagination** (Kerber Verlag, 2016), won the Eric Hoffer Award and the Nautilus Book Award.

The Artist's Curse – winner of a 2024 Silver Nautilus Book Award in the Creativity & Innovation category – distills more than twenty-five years inside the art world into the one thing it rarely teaches an artist: how to protect the self, liberate the imagination, and **remain free.**

stevesabella.space

The Artist's Curse
emaginity
Published in hardcover | softcover | ebook.
Spring 2023
ISBN 978-3-949392-17-7 (hardcover)
ISBN 978-3-949392-12-2 (paperback)
ISBN 978-3-949392-16-0 (ebook)

Cover image
Artwork by Cécile Elise Sabella

Assistant editor & proofreader
Cécile Elise Sabella

Design
Steve Sabella

www.stevesabella.space
linkedin.com/in/Steve-Sabella
instagram.com/Steve_Sabella

Thanks to Francesca Sabella for being part of this cosmic journey. Her **light** shines on every **cure**.

Thanks to Cécile for her sharp eyes and the cover's eternal **beauty**.

Thanks to Maggy Berloni, Gamal Abuali, Lily Farhoud Boullata, Hani Zurob, Najwan Darwish, Hendrik Backerra Michael Neuwirth and Fatema Ghadieh Asfour.

Thanks to Dr. Basel Dalloul & Wafa Roz for believing in **education**.

Thanks to everyone who was involved in this project through the years.

Thanks to **Metroquadroarte Gallery** for supporting the book in its earlier stages.

Publication is sponsored by the **Dalloul Art Foundation**

life.

"Being is a dream within a dream. All existence is but an imagination within the **imagination.**" Ibn Arabi.

A journalist once called me for an interview in Arabic for an exhibition he couldn't attend but still wished to write something about. Since all the PR material was in English, the journalist double-checked **my name in Arabic.** Instead of spelling it out, I said it once, twice, till I thought he heard it right. Even though he wondered whether Steve Sabella was my actual name, I assured him it was. The next day, he featured the article with the title,

"Artist Saif Zaballah opens his new exhibition Kan Yama Kan."

Saif Zaballah

is Arabic for

The Garbage Sword.

This joke

taught me to ask journalists to send my studio the articles to double-check the facts. As for the critique, as curse 157 tells you, **it's none of your business.**

It's about **quality and not quantity.** In the world of art, it matters who speaks about you. In the same way, it also matters which publisher, gallery, or curator you work with.

Decisions you made in the past do not get lost or forgotten through time. One day, the consequences are bound to surface. Be aware of your actions and their echoes as you choose where to exhibit, who you work with, and what statements you release.

Remember,

Despite shifting sea tides, the waves will **always be there.**

CURSE 192–THE COMMITMENT

Sometimes life takes you on a detour to teach you one more thing about yourself. If you feel some projects require more time than you calculated, so be it. The art journey is not a calculation but a process, and no matter what direction you choose, **you are always learning**.

CURSE 193–THE REALITY CHECK

You know smoking will kill you, but you will only stop when you become aware it will after a fatal diagnosis.

Knowing you are an artist, and becoming aware that you are one, will inject you with clarity and life.

Relaxed in a club once with my friends, a random guy sat beside me, insisting on knowing my age. And when I finally answered that I was 40, he said,

"I am **30** now,
and at **40**,
I want to be you.
Teach me."

I answered,

"Lesson 1:
When you become 40,
your only aim is
to **become you.**
Not me."

An artist in her twenties came to my studio feeling angry and frustrated after attending a forum on the art market. She had learned nothing new about promoting her work to collectors.

Collectors need to see you and your work.
Discover you.

Think of the channels to showcase your art. They could be with galleries, online, reviews in newspapers and magazines, social media, and many others. If your art is not there, how do you expect people to buy it? **So make your art visible. Discoverable.**

Once, after a TV aired a 30-minute documentary on my work, one of the most prominent collectors called me, and I closed a sale of $40,000.

Be out there.

CURSE 196–THE ARTIST'S GRAMMAR

Unlike novels, art's **visual syntax** does not follow a linear pattern.

There is no starting point to looking at an artwork. We can view it from **any direction**.

Great artists master their visual syntax, creating infinite readings of their work.

CURSE 197—THE MISSING THEORY

As an artist, focus on your art. Let others find the theory behind your creations.

Does it happen that you look at a painting and feel it was **overdone?**

How often do you read a novel feeling the writer should have toned it **down?**

How frequently do you watch a film and think that the actors or the director overplayed some scenes throwing you **off?**

Achieve harmony by looking at your art as if it was the work of others. Leave it to breathe alone for days or weeks, and when you come back to it, you will judge the creation **better.**

Your dreams become a reality when you **wake up** and start working.

OTHERWISE,

it's a waste of your time, sleep, and imagination.

When I felt all doors and windows shut before me once, questioning the essence of my art and life, I received these words:

Hello Steve,

Very happy to hear you're well and that our journey will continue soon! I don't want to steal much of your time this weekend, but there is something I would love to share right away.

As I wrote, I wanted to dive deeper into your artistic journey, and I started by watching all those videos that had English subs, and I must say these interviews and the things I saw and what you said range among the most inspiring words or works I encountered in **my life.**

My thoughts just went away to space and back when I learned more about you, some of your perspectives, your wounds, how you stitched them, and how you expressed yourself, your experiences, and your growth, development, **metamorphosis, and liberation.**

And how you shared all of that with the world. And how all of that interacts with the world and resonates in me. I am deeply impressed.

And there was what you said about these few things where only one perspective is possible. Rape, torture and occupation, the absolute worst among **man-made trauma.**

I had collected so much information and inspiration from you and your journey that I started to interrogate myself once more, but from **another perspective.**

And I was looking for what we have in common in our ways of liberating ourselves. And what we had in common that created that strong desire and need for liberation in the first place - and what made desire so strong became a driving force behind our lives (if not THE driving force - at least for quite some time).

It was mind-blowing.

We both went on to heal from the wounds we took, but we did this in a very very different way, only to then end up with quite similar conclusions and lessons learned - and a good understanding of freedom and liberation.

I really benefit on a personal level from your perspectives because what I was never able to do - or not in that scale, depth and impact like you - was actually sharing what I learned.

Sharing the knowledge and help to liberate minds. This is something that you - in my humble opinion - mastered, so you can imagine how inspiring that is for me...

I am still learning so many things, still always searching, without really knowing what for, but meeting you was, is, and will forever remain a wonderful gift.

I thank you (and the universe) for that. Enjoy your weekend my friend, take care and keep on being so inspiring and liberating.

Stefan

The theorist, critic, and philosopher Walter Benjamin said at the beginning of the 20th century,

"The illiterate of the future will not be the man who cannot read the alphabet, but the one who cannot take a photograph."

A century later, the illiterate of the future will not be people who cannot take or read images but those who cannot understand or operate software–the program.

The day will come when we won't differentiate between **man and machine,**
illusion and reality,
a program and free thought.

As an artist, equip yourself to handle much software that powers your creation. And as the world moves to digital and virtual reality, it has never been more crucial to

adjust, **adapt** or vanish.

The art market is unregulated, allowing genius fraud and money laundering. Only time will reveal the scope of such scandals. One day we might discover many masterpieces were made by master forgers, making them **the real masters.**

In 2018, Étienne Terrus Museum in France discovered half of its collection was fake. The local mayor described the revelation as a

"**catastrophe**"

for the region. And after the announcement, experts started investigating if works by other regional artists in different locations might also be counterfeit. **Good luck!**

Don't underestimate the number of fakes in the art market. To protect your art after your departure to the afterlife, ensure you have a clear record of your originals, hence the catalog raisonné of curse 158, and decide early on how you authenticate your art.

If you think this only matters after you die, **think again.**

Galleries sometimes **pay artists monthly salaries.** In return, the artists commit to passing on all their creations or a fixed number of artworks to the gallery. The gallery then is in control of their market and can sell the artworks at the value they wish to collectors without giving the standard **50% commission.**

Artists agree to this equation because of financial stress, war, and relocation. If you find yourself in such a situation, and no other options are available to you, whatever contract you sign, make sure it has a limited time period, preferably as short as possible. Otherwise, you get locked and might lose the desire to

But never forget that you are not selling yourself but your art.

Sometimes you will feel there is **infinite** money in this world and sometimes **none**.

Depending on where you live, the number of schemes to help artists might surprise you. And some are really creative. In Germany, for example, some funds grant artists a salary of 2500 euros for one year and do not even ask artists to report how they spend them. This is because they realized that **artists become more productive** by relieving the daily stress of making ends meet. But they will only give it to you based on previous achievements and if the jury feels you were born an artist.

Research the grants in your country, where applicable, and put their **deadlines on your calendar** as yearly reminders. One successful grant or stipend can do wonders for your

There is always another way.

And one day, you might discover

the answer
right there
in front of
you.

Distancing ourselves from our problems allows for better decisions.

But how?

When I want a better answer, I imagine myself eighty years old, reflecting on my life now, asking myself,

"Now that I think about it, if I would return in time, I would have done this better."

You become more objective and creative in **solving what matters.**

During the **check-in,** the hotel receptionist said I was sharing the room with another artist. I sleep naked, snore like a tractor, and worship my personal space. Exhibiting in different countries for artists is not a holiday. It's loaded with stress, meetings, and many unexpected challenges. When I spoke to the curator, she said there was no budget for all artists to have a private room. **Excuse me!**

All
artists
exhibiting
in
the
same
show
are
equal.

In the art world,

success and failure are two sides of the **same coin,**

as mentioned in curse 83. But it can take artists an eternity to **embrace both.** And when they do, the spectators can only see in their failure a success story.

Art can do magic to the consciousness of people.

In 2005, a group of masked and armed men kidnapped me and my colleague in Gaza, holding us **hostage** for several hours. They wanted the release of a family member from prison. We were **breaking news** on many media channels, as it was the first kidnapping incident in Gaza. **They threatened to kill us in three hours** if their demands were not met. Isolated in a room surrounded by guns, I started speaking to the kidnapper next to me, warming up to him. Talking about life and art, I later passed on my card. Four years later, I received this email:

Dear Steve,

I hope you are in the best of health and in excellent condition. I sent you this letter to confirm my deep appreciation for your exhibitions and photos, which are very beautiful. And here I am, bringing back to your memory the kidnapping incident, a tragedy for you and Miss Constantine, that happened over three years ago in Gaza. I was one of its masterminds.

Since that day, I have been feeling guilty, even though you understood the motives and that you were not the target. Because of you, the life of a person was saved.

Having said that, I offer you and Miss Constantine my utmost apologies regarding the incident and ask for your forgiveness for any annoyance I have caused you both. I urge you to convey my apologies to Zoi Constantine if you have a way to contact her. I'm asking both of you to correspond with me and accept my apology because even though you forgave me during the incident, I have a feeling you did not forgive me deep inside your hearts.

The one who made an error,
F. Abed

Just as you would like it when you receive an email or compliments on your work,

tell others how you liked their movie, novel, or performance.

You never know when
it will reach them and
how your words impact their reality.
This approach can also help you grow your

There
are
**infinite
possibilities.**

Imagination, like infinity,
can never be measured,
which gives imagination

limitless power.

The 13th-century poet and mystic Rumi once wrote,

"Somewhere beyond right and wrong there is a garden. I will meet you there."

When I interview potential assistants, I challenge them with a scenario on how to go forward if I believe the studio should move in a specific direction whereas they think it should go in another. If they answer, "we compromise," it tells me something about the weakness of their decision making. They are missing **the reward of agreement** that leads to the best route to the garden.

My capacity to understand others increased when I learned to become more silent.

Pay attention to others, and they will pay attention to you.

What you do as an artist has **an impact.** I once exhibited and gave a talk at The Palestinian Museum in Palestine. I spoke about complex themes of exile, self interrogation, introspection, and liberation.

As my talk extended over the schedule a few minutes, you know how it is when the organizers at the very back signal you to end with their hands or by flashing a special light. Rushing to the end, skipping a few ideas, I apologized to the attendees if I stole any of their time. On the spot, **Yousef**, an 11-year-old boy sitting in the front seat with his mother, said in a passionate voice,

"I wish you spoke longer."

It shocked me that a kid entered my world and wanted to remain there.

A few days later, I asked to meet Yousef to give him an artwork and donated the art I exhibited to the museum to go for auction to benefit the museum's education program.

When you find out that you have no options left to borrow money from banks, family, or friends, **return to your canvas** and create art. It will find a magical way to carry you. This is how my artwork, **The Great March of Return,** entered a museum collection before I even finished it.

is you.

Unlucky are those who
do not see their **glitter.**

Not every collector or buyer of art likes to meet the artist. I know of collectors who disliked the artworks after meeting artists whose personalities they despised.

A gallerist once told me biennales are for artists and art fairs for galleries. The presence of artists in the booth or around it might be in the gallery's way.

When people love a work of art, they develop an image of its creator, and sometimes you might be better off remaining **an image.**

I once started a GoFundMe campaign titled The Patrons – Call to All Creatives raising almost $97,214 in six months. Little did I know then that

PATREON, a platform that connects patrons to artists, existed. Many artists have found Patreon the ideal way to find and engage with the right audiences, who get rewarded by creative tiers set up by the artists. **Patreon is not about selling art but about creating and liberating it, finding people who can support you from $1 monthly**. And imagine if you have thousands! Patreon gives power to the collective.

On Patreon you might realize that your friends are your last supporters, not willing to invest $12 on your creative journey per year. But, the good news, with proper marketing, you can reach a new audience and break free to focus on what matters to you the most.

For me, it didn't work, but it might be a perfect fit for you.

As I set up Patreon, I invited a person to my studio to discuss investing in one of my art projects. Knowing if we were a match was essential, as I work with people only when the visions are aligned. When he mentioned he was selling his company in the US for $10 million, I said without meaning to insult, but understanding the power of one,

"I can pay you **one** dollar."

He jumped in my face saying,

"Fuck You."

It was the second time we met and for sure the last time.

Galleries can sell your work **on consignment,** i.e., you get paid when the work is sold. If you are in a good relationship with the gallery, consignments are significant assets, as you can use them as collateral when needed to get a loan or a down payment.

Keep a clear inventory over the years. It's easy to lose track.

You think you will remember, **you won't.**

CURSE 221–THE BUSINESS OF LOOKING

There is art and there is **the art market.**

Everything has a price tag, but when a masterpiece is born, it becomes priceless.

CURSE 222–THE ART BUSINESS

Creating art and selling it are two different aspects of being an artist. Both involve creativity, but the latter requires an understanding of business. With the right knowledge and skills, you can make a living from selling your art. You already possess more knowledge than you think, so it's just a matter of honing those skills. **Just dare, like in curse 117, so you don't get lost in space.**

CURSE 223–THE WISH

It's not enough to **wish or dream** for things as curse 199, The Paradox shows you. You must **want** them. Otherwise, the wish remains in the clouds. Wanting something will give you more power to achieve your desires on **earth**.

CURSE 224–THE HARD NO

Sometimes knowing what you don't want might be more relevant than knowing what you want. Saying no to certain exhibitions, initiatives, or interviews might save your career, reputation, and life.

Over time, your intuition and knowledge will guide you to whether it should be a definite or painful

Yes or **No.**

The decisions you make are your future CV.

All artists are on different journeys, sailing in different directions, and it's futile to compare and **compete.**

Don't shy away from sharing your knowledge or your navigation of the art **world.**

Helping others is re**war**ding.

The curator's power lies in their gaze upon the world with a bigger picture in mind. They connect the unexpected, make sense, or confuse the order of the realities we live in. Yet, some curators might have it tough. If they are not superstars, sometimes their remuneration is cut, ignored, or dropped altogether.

They often publish their essays. But who can live off magazine or newspaper publications?

Today, you encounter curators who hook artists to galleries or arrange for big museum shows and, secretly or not, ask the artist and the representing galleries for a 5 to 10% commission. Share this percentage in a friendly spirit without thinking twice. **Or even once.**

Nothing

stays

the

same.

Foucault once said,

"I don't feel that it is necessary to know exactly what I am. The main interest in life and work is to become someone else you were **not in the beginning.**"

Some artists choose not to name their projects or artworks. The decision comes after failing to create a good name. When you feel lost, title the process you went through instead of naming single artworks. Here are the titles of all my projects from 1997 until I moved to London in 2007:

Search

Identity

End of Days

Till the End

Kan Yama Kan (**Once Upon a Time**)

Jerusalem in Exile

Exit

Mentalopia

You want people to find your work online. Search for Steve Sabella Till the End or Steve Sabella Untitled? What if you have many untitled artworks? It becomes a mess. And when your work appears at auctions, it won't sound terrific if many of your records are

untitled.

It leads people into your universe. It's a starting or an arresting point.

A title adds value to a work of art and helps your professional network identify your work and market it.

The **title**

usually emerges as you create the art. If not, notice the first words you use when describing your art to your family and friends.

And never forget **untitled** artworks will require more explanation from you.

Most artists dread writing them, and sometimes they take longer than the creation of the artwork itself. Yet, we can't escape them. A good way out is to converse with someone who will note your initial words. It's there where you could find your statement's first sentences.

A good statement
is like
a good melody.
If it hits your heart first,
it will echo
in the intellect.

So keep it **short** and **simple** while knowing that your art is the authentic statement.

Unless dynamic art market forces are beyond your control, don't raise the prices of your art too fast. **The last thing you want** later when demand drops is to lower them, creating speculation and uncertainty about your career.

The art world has **no mercy,**

and it could take years to develop a renewed confidence in your work. Instead, create smaller artworks that fit the concept of your oeuvre and price them

lower!

CURSE 233–THE SIGNATURE

SIGN all your

works after you finish them to identify them as yours. Add the creation date. If you are working with limited editions, inscribe the name, the number, the size, the year of creation, and other necessary information.

It will surprise you how many artists neglect this. Unsigned artworks will always have less value. For sure, **after you are gone.**

CURSE 234—THE ART FRAME AGAIN

Make it tempting to jump in. If lost, go to a major art fair intending to study how artists frame their art. The new insight will revive you and your art. I started working with matt diasec after seeing a show **by Gerhard Richter.**

Gallerists won't only judge your art but also the quality of your mounting and frames. Once a gallery was convinced to work with me after seeing the frames for my project, 38 Days of Re-Collection.

Awards, grants, curated exhibitions, reviews in media, books, monographs, auction records, interviews, documentaries, juried shows, biennales, museum collections, private & public collections, and for sure social media success **all contribute to increasing the value of your art.**

CURSE 236–THE BREVITY

Brevity is an art.

I used to write long emails, losing people's attention. When you write to anyone about your work, always be brief at the start. **It's not a love letter.** People are busy, and I know of a collector and a lawyer who only read the first two lines.

CURSE 237–THE WEBSITE

Your website is your home or global base, where you can be in control of its design and features. A stellar website serves you like the studio visit of curse 124, The Magic Carpet. Make it **stand out.**

In a healthy art environment, the gallery is **the artist's home base,** where the art price enjoys stability and the artist receives close attention. The gallery reacts rationally to supply and demand and auction house frenzies. But you will also find galleries that conspire with auction houses, fixing the value of the art by bidding on it. Auction house sales are always discreet unless the buyer does not care to disclose the name.

The art market is unregulated, allowing for many practices and schemes. However, what is real or not depends on who's telling **the story.**

Any creation stands out when its creator becomes invisible.

We love to read a story where we replace the author's voice with ours. We love to see a movie where we don't feel the director but feel immersed in the scene. Likewise, a poem works best when freed from **its narrator.**

It's YOU.

Start working.

Step **by** Step

Time
will
teach
all
you
need.

Unless you are super lucky, you won't find patrons to support you without offering them something in return. Everyone likes to get something. When you want to deal with patrons, make it serve their interest so that you have better chances of getting their support.

Try.

Most people try things till they don't work. Trying lacks will. Success will happen when you are persistent,

Don't try. **Act.**

And don't forget **the strongest** word that has the power to change all realities, as curse 66 reveals.

It hits everyone. But don't panic—give your block a visual form in the worst-case scenario.

The only way to start is to start.

All masterpieces began with their first stroke. Whether you're reading or writing, all books start with the first word, and before you know it, words turn into lines, paragraphs into pages, and pages into the complete story.

Don't make your life an ongoing trial of pushing a car uphill. When it feels too heavy, let go or move aside. Sometimes, a crash is an opportunity to start **from scratch**—and of course, to buy a new car.

I never went to an art residency because I never found the time and didn't want to leave my family alone for an extended period. However, prestigious residences help connect you to many people in the art world. They give you the space to

work
on
new art,

explore different cities and cultures in the world, and keep you engaged. If you can, aim to **do one every two years.**

All art originates from reflections on the past which artists later express in every possible way. Since art deals with **your history**, the hours you spend working on art will make you feel better. The past cannot be changed, but you can change your perception of it. This is when you **find your inner peace.**

Through art, one can heal the self and **others.**

Getting **angry,**

anxious,

and depressed is natural and is part of life. What's not natural is to remain locked in these states.

When things happen around you not to your liking, the only thing in your **control** is your reaction, the real action that will define **who you are** to yourself and to others.

TREASURE the people who understand you.

They are like guiding stars in your cosmic art journey.

If anyone spends a year studying any topic out of desire, that person will become an expert in that field.

Compare two scholars: one doing a master's program at a top university, working part-time, and preparing for exams, and another who does not seek the stress of the degree and engages

in self

education.

Who will gain more knowledge at the end of that year?

A focused week or month can also do its **magic.**

Visual art is
transformed light,
and each artist does
this transformation in
their own way. And
since no one knows
the origin of light,
art will always reveal
mystic layers,
renewing itself in
endless formations
and
constellations.

For some people,

art is only an investment, **nothing** more.

Many galleries fear you sell directly to collectors. It's never in your interest to do so, even though **the temptation** of saving the 50% gallery commission is high. The art world is small, and the deal's details will inevitably come out.

When you get an inquiry from anyone to buy your work, ask where they saw it and how they found you. Once you find the trace, refer the buyers to your gallery. You will **gain credibility**, and don't be dazzled when the gallery focuses more on promoting your work from that point on. Your aim should be about creating a sustainable art career, not on one sale that can help you **now.**

Sell independently only when there are **no conflicts of interest.**

The only way to prevent pulling your hair from its roots, to find time to shower, eat, **call** your doctor, or **your shrink,** catch up with friends, **sleep,** and believe there is a tomorrow is to set your date without **death** embedded in it. Don't wait till the last moment. Only then will you complete your tasks without killing your-**self.**

At an art fair, a collector once said he preferred artworks he could recognize like a brand.

History has shown us that great collectors are the curious ones, those who buy with their eyes, not their minds, those who **discover** and challenge themselves. Those who fall in love. Following a brand is a waste of taste. And the collectors might be missing what's happening underground.

It takes time for new styles to **sink in.** Think of the impressionists, the cubists, or the surrealists. It only requires a few daring artists to have a movement attracting a few bold collectors. History rewards those who **dare.**

Many collectors complain about the value-added tax on buying art. In some countries, it's **another 25%** on the sales price.

They expect the gallery or artist to **suck it up.** VAT is a legal requirement, but to adjust, dealers have found ingenious ways to evade it, like postponing the sale until an art fair is over and then invoicing the collector at an address not subject to local tax by shipping it to a VAT-exempt country. This or that way, ensure your papers are correct to prevent paying later not only the VAT but a hefty fine too.

And now, as the world moves digital, cryptocurrency might be the new cash of the **black** market.

Don't be alarmed if the agent's commission ranges from 0% to 50%. **Zero** to draw you in and facilitate the first deal, and 50% for very confident agents. **See 20-25% as a good negotiation percentage.**

You quickly learn that most agents only work with mid-range to high-end art sales. One agent stopped working with me after securing a decent commission, enough to buy herself a flat in Paris. Thanks to **the Cubists.**

Don't shy away from inviting people who love you and your work to invest in your creations.

If you work independently, you are in theory saving the 50% gallery commission, which you can use as an incentive and leverage to **reward your supporters**. Entice them by giving them art at 30-50% off as if waving the gallery commission. You get the budget you need for your next project, and they get the art they like at a great value, becoming for them a safer investment.

Or, if your supporters don't wish to buy your art, offer them the money back with a decent agreed return, effective after the first sale of any artworks in the series. Once it works the first time, don't be surprised when they contact you enquiring about

your **next** project.

I once created

The Membership Model, which **aimed to** entice ten collectors to acquire one artwork per year for three years, **and in return,** I guaranteed them **a permanent 30% discount and one artwork as a gift.**

I wanted to free my time to **focus solely on my art.**

Some galleries have great experience deciding who to sell your art to so that it does not end up in the hands of a speculator who buys for investment, quickly flipping artworks to auction houses, an **arbitrage** purely **about money**. Neither galleries nor artists like their works to end up in an auction through this route. The artwork may not get sold at all, and to protect the artist, galleries often repurchase the artwork to **save its value.**

Or, the artwork could sell many times more than its upper estimate, affecting the value of all your art. If your art gets caught in an investment bubble, and you don't find creative ways to sustain your art's value over time, there is nowhere but to go down with the prices of your work to survive. And this is the last thing you want to do because people will trust **your art less.**

So, if you work independently, be careful who you sell to, as once the artwork leaves your studio, it has a life and **a market of its own.**

CURSE 259–THE MISSING CURSE

Some art fairs offer artists space to sell their work directly. If you want to do it on your own, consider the following:

The size of the space you need, its price, the lights, their number, their function, and their distance from the walls. Do you want your floor carpeted? White walls or color? Is your booth titled or not? Which font, what size? Bring a toolbox or hire professionals at the fair? Do you have **enough money?**

Do you have insurance? Did you think of storage space, a cupboard to lock your valuables and catalogs after you rest or party at night? Most likely, there won't be internet, but you can order a modem at the fair, which will only work if you have an electrical plug. One more thing to sort out. Unless the cupboard you ordered can fit **bags of cash,** you might need to consider renting a credit card machine for **faster payments.**

And when the **VIP opening** starts, you ask yourself why you didn't offer Champagne, just like the gallery across from you. Then, when you realize the cost is 12 euros per glass, you will

understand why.

The most complicated are return shipments, local tax, customs, and VAT. But all this is a waste of effort if you don't do your homework, attracting the attention of collectors and museums alike beforehand, as suggested in the curse you read before or

the headache

If you ask me, **accept the 50% gallery** commission in return for their work so that you focus on your art. And don't forget to say **thank you.**

There is a chance you will never see your exhibited works again. For years, I had pending shipments from two exhibitions. When I inquired, the organizers said they were waiting for the green light for a new show or looking for a new budget to transport them back. If you would take matter into your own hands, we all know how much it could cost to ship art **across continents.**

This explains why artworks got **lost in history** and how they resurfaced in the most bizarre ways. Just make sure the agreements are clear about the return of your art. And always **follow up.**

Galleries can never represent all artists. There are way more artists than galleries.

Represented or not, aim to build a list of your own collectors and show your work on online channels to keep attracting new eyes. In your career, you will discover that your friends will become more and more interested in what you do, and they will start acquiring.

No book,
lecture,
workshop, or
seminar can give you all the answers.

The answer is in your mind
and how you connect the dots.
And don't assume that success is
about making money off your art.

TIME
will teach you
where
the real **value** is.

If you are looking for a book to widen your perspectives and imagination, find The Power of **Myth** by Joseph Campbell, who saw art as a landscape for the soul and artists as **the new shamans.**

He researched how art connects directly to **the soul**, seeing artists as mediators. So if someone says that your art helped them or changed their lives, see this as your biggest reward.

Even though many artists transform their psychological states into visual forms, it doesn't matter how they relate to their art and why they create. For example, do we care now what triggered or inspired

The Four Seasons

by Vivaldi?

In art, what eventually matters is the quality of the produced visuals and their **contribution to life.**

Doing other jobs to survive as you find your way in the art world is not a shame. On the contrary, they will only strengthen you and make you wiser. I know of a 22-year-old artist from Istanbul who fled the city because of nudity in her art. To survive, she chops wood twice a week in a Berlin forest. I met a musician who worked in construction for a few years until he figured things out.

If you see your actions as part of the journey towards the bigger picture of your life and art, you will be fine.

Nothing can stop a creative artist.

And as many will tell you, art is not work.

FACT:

only a few people will ever see your art in real.

So, have top-quality images of your art when shared online or in print. When needed, hire professionals. In London, the gallery I worked with hired a photographer to document every exhibition using a large digital format, Hasselblad. The images were a knock-out, almost triggering me to ask the photographer to travel to all my shows in Europe.

Don't underestimate the quality of the smartphones of today.

If you order your art sales history and inventory online, always make sure you download a backup to your computer. You never know when a company goes bust, risking losing all **your records.**

Online cataloging makes running the business of art way more manageable, especially as you grow in your career and your sales become in the tens and hundreds.

CURSE 269—THE PRESS DOCUMENTATION

When your work gets reviewed anywhere, create quality PDFs which you can **post on social media,** your website, and your newsletter. Today's programs allow you to order the PDF as you like, removing unnecessary clutter from online sources.

CURSE 270—THE VISUALIZATIONS

We live in a world of images, so cut your text and **improve your visuals.**

When you finish a project and want to introduce it, especially on social media, visualize your art as if exhibited in space instead of only showing the artwork's image. This way, people get a better feel of its **size and texture.**

Some publishers, journals, or academics may ask you for a bibliography, a list of works such as books, articles, reviews, and other publications on your art.

Create a spreadsheet to add your bibliography and **keep it updated.** It's only a lot of work if you neglect it. For example, my first monograph publisher requested everything from the 1990s to 2014. It took my studio weeks to prepare this document, filling several pages. Anyone researching your art would find this data valuable.

And the good news is that many websites offer you free citation help. Sometimes, all you have to do is post the ISBN number to receive:

Amelunxen, H. and Boullata, K., 2014. Steve Sabella Photography 1997-2014. Ostfildern: Hatje Cantz.

You are only selling the physical artwork, not its **copyright.**

Museums, collectors, and all others need your permission if they professionally use the artwork's image in books, magazines, TV, and so on. And as you know by now, agencies like DACS (curse 165) help you **receive the royalties.**

If you are confident about your artistic career and want to **focus only on creativity,** free your time by applying for a bank loan to cover your expenses for a set period.

If $2000 are your monthly expenses, see how many months you wish to cover. One year is refreshing, but six and three months can do wonders. The time you spend being creative will lead you to find organic ways to power the next period of your life, whether from a sudden sale of your new art, the perfect grant, prize, or residency. You pay back the loan in comfortable installments, which, trust me, you will handle. Just **imagine what you can do in that year!**

The trick is to receive the money and not worry about earning more as if you created **your own stipend.**

If your monthly expenses are $2000, and you get $20,000 from a sale and not a bank loan, transfer the amount to a special account and give yourself **a salary of $2000 monthly.**

Like this, you will clear your mind to focus on creativity for ten months. If the sale is $6000, divide it into three months. You get the idea. And if you earn an extra income during this period, you will feel you have extra money to **do the things you love.**

I should have learned this lesson when I sold art for over $50,000 more than once. Instead, I spent the money without consideration for this safety net, leading to

the next **curse**.

If your income is too high, it will be subject to higher income tax. Often, the difference between one taxed category and the next is high. If you were not paying attention and filing regularly, you might owe income **tax money you don't have.**

To lower your profit margin, invest in tax-deductible things like studio materials, equipment, and software. Even travel and business dinners qualify as expenses.

A good **accountant** will provide you with the best advice on needed purchases toward the end of the tax year and sometimes before if they find your income too high. They are also best for handling tax auditing, which will **inevitably** happen **to you.**

Pay them on time. Once in a meeting with an **income tax collector,** she was super clear in her answer when I said I also had to honor monthly payments to health insurance and banks. She asserted,

"You pay us first."

Otherwise, they can confiscate your bank account, paralyzing your life and workflow.

To **avoid this trauma**, save a percentage of your income in a different account, untouchable unless **really** needed.

Aim to have art lawyers in your **circle** of friends. You never know when you need professional advice and **a reduced bill.** Most disputes are solvable without going to court. And if required, many lawyers could see value in your art and accept it as payment, unlike your banks, unless you are super established or a blue-chip artist.

CURSE 278–THE ARTIST'S NETWORK

You are more likely to get noticed by curators, collectors, and galleries if you interact with other artists' networks who invite you to their openings or simply recommend you. Many artists entered major exhibitions or prestigious collections because of such **random connections.**

Help others, and others will help you. Don't compete. Through synergy, you achieve much more.

CURSE 279–THE LINKED IN

Engaging with the social network LinkedIn is your fastest way to bring your name forward to people who matter, like gallery owners, curators, museum directors, and collectors, as you can connect to them and even send direct messages. Use it creatively and professionally. Like this, **your network can grow while sitting on your studio chair.**

CURSE 280—THE CREATIVE MARKETING

If you want to boost your sales, earn more and make your art visible, learn the art of marketing. **Marketing is the secret** ingredient of all successful artists.

Don't wait to get discovered if you can find faster ways to reach people. And today, social media has made the world a smaller place.

CURSE 281—THE BARRIER

In 1995, artists Christo and Jeanne-Claude showed us that **nothing is impossible**. They wrapped the Reichstag government building in Berlin with 100,000 square meters of silver fabric. Described by the press as the couple's **"most spectacular achievement,"** know that it was years of work and many **rejections.**

When things don't work out, or you think it's all over, it is actually the beginning of

something

new,

time for the reset button,

for better learning,

getting more ready for your next

adventure.

Finally, you can have a domain with these endings, which look much better on your art card, and when you verbally share them:

Steve Sabella **. com**

or

Steve Sabella **. art**
Steve Sabella **. space**
Steve Sabella **. studio**

If you don't choose your name as your domain, make it simple and **easy to remember.**

CURSE 284—THE TAKEAWAY GIFT

People love to receive gifts from artists. **Give anyone who visits your studio something to help them remember you.** Art cards, catalogs, and monographs can do wonders for you later. More than once, people I interacted with years earlier **reappeared in my universe.**

CURSE 285—THE CONDITION

Some foundations and government bodies support only non-profit organizations or institutions, not individuals. But this does not mean you cannot apply for their funding.

Any non-profit institution you know and believe in can apply in your name. This means you create your project under their umbrella.

Also, this means you get endorsed twice.

The Artist's Curse tells you what needs to be done, but it's up to you how to **do it.**

Sometimes, you might need to resort to private funding to start or complete projects to speed things up. Approach people you know who have the ability. In return, offer them the money back, with profit if you wish, upon the first sale. Some would want to choose an artwork instead, and if so, clearly give them a discount. If you have a gallery representation, know that

no gallery would stand in your way if your close friends want to support you.

Don't forget to acknowledge everyone's support including the gallery in publications.

CURSE 288–THE CURATOR'S GIFT THAT WORKS

To **strengthen your critical acclaim,** research the curators you want to work with and send them a short message about why you like their work and why yours fit their vision, asking them if they would accept a catalog, a portfolio, a monograph, or whatever you wish. I did this in the past, landing me in grand exhibitions.

Where to find them and their contacts? See curses 278 & 279 and **start working.**

CURSE 289–THE ART OF NEGOTIATION

Everyone negotiates.

It's rare that you will ever sell one artwork without some sort of compromise on the original price. There are techniques to help you **improve**. Learn them.

Through self-publishing and print-on-demand, you can create, print, distribute, and sell your book at a fraction of the associated mainstream publishing costs. The options are many. **The world is changing, change with it.** You can make excellent catalogs of your work, even hardcovers. The idea is to get your work out there, visible in the different channels of curse 195.

Signed art books make exceptional gifts for **your studio visits.**

Enjoy every step of the journey. It can take years and decades to establish a sustainable art career.

Your **baby steps** today will one day become

You can still make it big time without gallery representation. It's a different route, and today, **the roads to success are endless.**

Waiting on something for something else to start is an attitude that leads to stillness and stagnation. When you start the action, the entire universe will conspire to help get you where you want.

As Joe Dispenza always says,

The dancer of life feels every vibration is a creative impulse.
Be the sound wave you want to hear.

The dancer of life
is you.

Continue creating **until the last breath.**

Artist Kamal Boullata passed away while sketching art on his bed. He left weeks before he saw the publication of his two books, whose titles alone reveal **the greatest symphony of life:**

There
Where
You
Are
Not

Uninterrupted Fugue

Novelist E. L. Doctorow once wrote,

"Writing a novel is like driving a car at night. You can see only as far as your **headlights,** but you can make the whole trip that way."

As an artist, you don't have to see your destination, but you can **get there step by step.** But knowing where you are going will give you the confidence you need to succeed.

When we stop **thinking of time** and **history** in a linear way, images become like time machines, vehicles of time able to transport us to any dimension. We create our own journeys, journeys into the imagination where everything we

imagine becomes a reality.

Stormy days erupt not only to shake you but also to clear for you **a new path.**

Remember the **murky waters** of curse 113 and **keep swimming!**

Depending on where you live, you must check this inconvenient truth which requires **clarity and action.** Otherwise, the people you leave behind might be subject to paying a hefty sum on the value of your **unsold art.**

First, get legal tax advice to write your will and sign it with a notary to remove any doubt. In some countries, it's not given that only your spouse, partner, or kids inherit you. It could include other members of your family, even those you never cared about. Failure to put a plan in place, the right people in charge, a charity, whatever you decide, will threaten **your legacy** if this is something you care about.

When I lived in London, I registered my business as a limited liability company with shares so that in case I died, all the art remained in the company, with my partner owning all shares. Then, I dissolved the company in Berlin and ran it as a sole proprietor, meaning I should inject this curse immediately and do **my f**king will**.

The Artist's **Cure.**

As

long as

there is one

person left who

imagines a better

world, **life has a chance.**

CURSE 303—THE SECRETS OF LIFE II

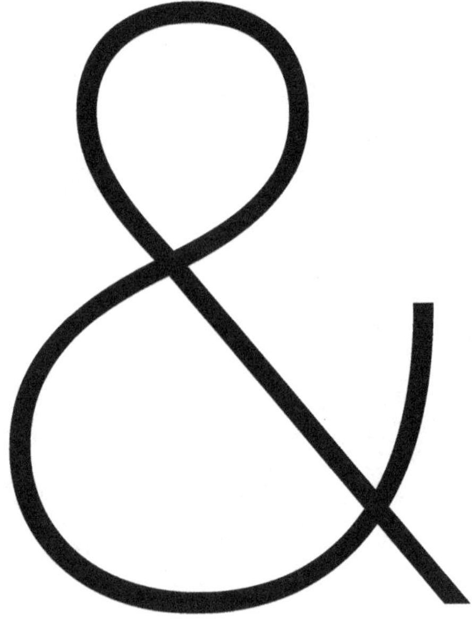

The **&** in curse 304 stands for addition and **participation.**

You will enjoy the **endless cosmic dance** when you become an active participant, adding to what's already **out there**.

Art is a great channel to look at our past, present, and future. At the beginning of the Corona reality, as the world went through a reset, **a restart,** and a new order, I asked a friend what she thought would happen. She answered, creatives

Never forget that the story of art is the story of life.

It's the end of something and the beginning of something else.

And because no one knows what this else is about, we might as well imagine new realities. The time has come for clarity, for all creatives to become super

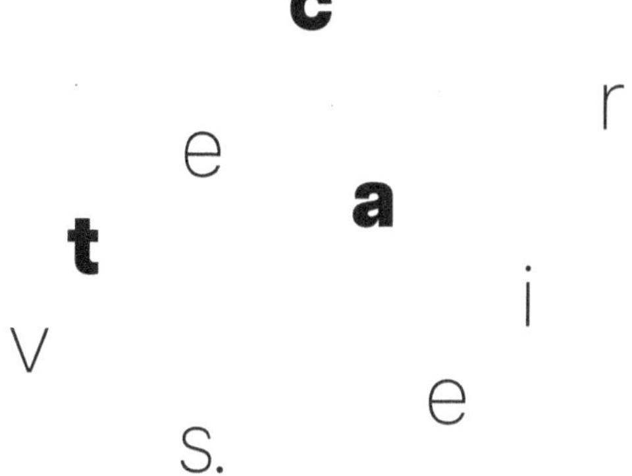

It matters like the first impression. If you choose to stop to work with certain galleries, institutions, collectors, or any art professionals, or if they stop working with you, do your best to **close the chapter in good spirits.**

As the art world moves to digital shows, virtual reality, and the selling of NFTs, people will feel the difference between **image and reality,** between the image of art and the 'real' artworks they can hang on their walls.

Keep
creating.

There can never be **one truth,**
one reality, but endless
variations. And the more you
dig into life, the deeper
your vision becomes.

With better seeing, doing the art is only a translation, the act of registration or transformation. When you see the artwork in your mind's eye, you can manifest it without effort

in the
blink of
an **e**y**e**.

The more art you do,
the more alive you are.
Design your reality.

From
nothing,
everything
starts,
everything
s**park**s**.**

It's an intimate experience to see where your artworks hang in their new homes. After a tour of a collector's house that ended in the bedroom, the collector said that she and her partner woke up every morning seeing the artwork in **a new way.** The artwork is a photo collage of my four-year-old daughter looking through a window in London.

Feeling her connection to the work, she had her own words about its meaning and context. It was no longer relevant that I was the work's creator, even feeling that my presence violated this sacred space. I couldn't wait to step out of the room.

See curse 9 on the life of the artwork's image and **free yourself.**

Be and let **be**.

The new space frontiers.

It's a virtual world where users or players can buy land, build spaces, and sell anything you can imagine. See it as **a parallel world,** an extension of what is already out there, except in this one, **only those ahead will be the best game players.**

Major galleries have already acquired virtual locations, and this new playground will become a fertile land for digital art, including NFTs.

Such spaces can grow your audience. Thinking that it won't be for you is akin to how many felt about joining Facebook when it launched. Look where we are today. **The show must go on!**

CURSE 315–THE GALLERIST

I once read that a dealer will send the collector an invoice, whereas a gallerist will send the collector an artist's biography.

CURSE 316 – THE TRICK

For people to appreciate your old works, **create new ones.**

Archaeology of the future
is archaeology of the image.

It's time to **dig deeper** into the genealogy of the image to better understand our origin and where we are heading.

What you seek,
seeks you.

It's not a secret that what you visualize manifests itself in its own way in reality. But you need to want it, as curse 223 The Wish reveals.

All this talk about finding one's **voice** has always amazed me.

Don't look for something that is **already there.** Your voice is who you are right now, and how you express yourself will always carry your **mark.**

The way you see the world is unique to you. Start from that angle, and you will always be original.

Tell your story with your own words, paint strokes, or musical notations.

Nobody will tell your story better than you.

The voice is you.

The universe has no wrong answers.

If the universe has no wrong answers, such awareness makes you accept any situation, connecting it to

the bigger picture of **life.**

Greek for **everything flows.**

Remember cure 184.
It is what it is, and it can be whatever it wants to **be.**

It is exactly
where you are.

I no longer reveal my formal education in daily talks. Instead, if asked, I answer that I have learned at:

The University of **Life**, where there are no alumni, only students, forever learning.

There was a time when the royals and the churches paid for connecting heaven and earth–the **Medici family** and the Vatican.

There was a time when everything collectors touched turned to **gold**–Peggy Guggenheim and Charles Saatchi.

There was a time when curators and galleries turned artists into market **stars**–The list is too long.

The time will soon come when auction houses turn artworks, possibly NFTs, into a one billion dollar commodity–
Christie's or Sotheby's?

Nobody wants to work in sickness. If you fall ill, the best cure will be to transform your illness into art. It will keep you alive, and don't be surprised when **it heals you.**

Everything I learned was from scratch. **Ok,** maybe I had a bit of talent.

That's only true because I see myself as a geek, often buying a dozen books on the same topic. Artists learn and develop as they go. That's the beauty of it.

Composing the symphony of your life comes after years of practice, but it starts by learning **the first note.**

I suffered from depression for a long time. And I got out of it. I even forgot when—a good sign it worked.

The feeling of paralysis goes away once you engage with life again. Any movement is an antidote to depression. And this does not include moving your eyes on your living room couch, day and night. This is fine as long as you know that stillness is a state of movement. The world is always moving. So keep creating. Go out. Do whatever. Find your drawing board, or even break it. Make depression the core of **your art.**

The change of air of curse 143 always helps. If you can, leave your country and live anywhere else, even for a few days or weeks. Waking up to find out where to get your bread, have a drink, and figure out your needs adds color to your life. And before you know it, you are

Never wait for external factors to change so that something can change in you. You can read all the guru books and listen to anyone, but change only happens if

executed by

you.

CURSE 331–THE BAD ART

I learned more from watching lousy art and films than from seeing great ones. I learned how not to do it.

CURSE 332–THE MISSED ENERGY AND THE RESTART

When you start a project, **finish it.**

What you could complete now in seven days could take seven months in the future. The story of The Artist's Curse! But it also means you will do it better. And console yourself by the revelation of curse 321, **the universe has no wrong answers.**

CURSE 333—THE DISCRIMINATION

There are no "artists of color."
There are only **artists.**

The term itself is
racist.

CURSE 334—THE MUSEUM'S COMMISSION

Accept museum commissions when they are part of your visual journey and less because you need the money. This is when you will do them from your heart. Otherwise, you will create **contrived** and **dry art.**

What people see as 'the sudden success' or 'the big break' is often the work of many years. Over time, you become more creative in solving problems, speeding up your **progress.**

Life is short,
but your art career is long
and will inevitably go
through many stages.
The best way to remain
empowered on the stage is to
take care of yourself.

A non-fungible token, or **NFT**, can only give more value and aesthetics to physical art, making it a non-replaceable and desired asset. NFT is revolutionary, upgrades the concept of collectables, and rewards artists for their creativity through endless artist resale rights. But, it has created a wave of fake attributes to artwork images.

Pak's NFT project "The Merge" sold for $91.8 million in 2021, surpassing Jeff Koons's Rabbit, which sold at Christie's in 2019 for **$91,075,000.**

In the world of art, nothing is im**possible.**

As the world moves digital, space becoming virtual, and art assets non-fungible, physical galleries will become less relevant, replaced by online platforms, which will become more profitable and favorable **Develop your online presence and maintain its quality.**

Sometimes, the biggest obstacle in your career is **your ego.**

The best description of ego I read was its manifestation as a **balloon.**

Pierce it, **and** it's gone.

Misunderstandings inevitably happen between you and people. We often misread messages or emails, judging others. People have different interpretations to words. You can clear things up by email or texting, but picking up the phone and hearing a voice on the other side helps clear the air. It brings something human back and lets you better **feel what needs to be done or said.**

I once told my daughter that there are a few people you need to choose well in your life: your hairdresser, your dentist, your lawyer, your general doctor, and your accountant. And, of course, **your partner.**

I fell into a trap when I lived in the UK, hiring an accountant who did not file on time or even understand the nature of the art business. I later learned that people can be accountants in the UK without proper certification.

The next accountant I hired cost me a fortune to fix the mistakes of the first. And if you think I learned my lesson when I moved to live in Berlin, **think again.**

The Berlin accountant underestimated my career, where I suddenly owed income tax a hefty sum, even though I had fully paid my quarterly installments. You can imagine the strength needed to fix it, leading me to go public with a GoFundMe Campaign and even appear **on TV.**

Once you become more established, you will get asked more than once a year to donate an artwork here and there. If you go for it, check if you can **make the donation tax-deductible.**

Ask your accountant.
Not mine.

Don't fear your death, but the mess you could leave behind. Your journey ends on earth, and who knows what's after. But one thing is for sure, you can **make life easy for those who care about you.**

Consult with a lawyer about leaving a will and the legalities. They are different in each country. After your death, those who loved you and those who didn't might enter **legal wars.** Leave a clear trace of where you store your art and who has it on consignments or loans. If you did not do proper homework, the art might be subject to inheritance tax, creating

a **nightmare.**

The more information you keep on the ownership of your art, consignments, and your method of art authentication, the easier you make it for your estate to protect your art and legacy. The key to achieving this is to **remain organized**, informing at least one person how and where to access information.

In brief, you can curate your legacy and set its foundation. And if you can, create a charitable art foundation. Many artists will love you.

The more you **see**
the invisible, the less
you will surrender to reality.
We create our own reality.

Life is
as we
imagine
it.

Many people search for their purpose in life, many never finding it, a quest that adds stress and disappointment. **Why settle for one purpose?** Having multiple purposes grants you better **chances.**

This is how the world should be.

When **confused,**
consult your heart.
It will always give you
a better answer.

The
only
way
forward
is
forward.

expect nothing in return.

Life has its own memory, and one day, you will not believe how something worked out for you.

Dream big

and

keep planting seeds

in

the quantum universe.

You will never know
when and how
they flourish.

I once read that "If the laws of the financial world applied to the art world, **everybody** would be **in prison**: the collectors, the gallerists, the artists, the critics, the museum directors, and the people who run the auction houses."

Stefan Sagmeister in "100 Secrets of the Art World"

CURSE 352–THE RELIEF

Cherish yourself and your friends,

not money.

This is where you will find absolute splendour.

CURSE 353 – THE NEW WAYS

As artists, we can always tread the paved roads of the art world, but we can constantly create parallel routes.

It is only in this uncharted territory where **the magic happens.**

In art lies power feared by political systems and movements for only one reason: It allows for **self-liberation.** One freed individual defeats all weapons.

The Colonization of the Imagination.

There is an Other in all of us.

Each

Other.

The time has come to stop drawing borders and start **drawing our future.**

It is always in you.
Accept what's
coming to you,
and mirror it all
out.

After drowning many times, I learned this from Alan Watts:

"To have faith is to trust yourself to the water. When you swim, you don't grab hold of the water because if you do, you will sink and drown. Instead, you **relax and float.**"

When
everything
collapses,
remember that
zero is a
good place to

start.

The state of nothing is
the state of all creation.

CURSE 360—THE POWER OF NOTHING

When you think you are nothing or have nothing, just know that you have everything in you to **start again.**

CURSE 361—ARTISTS DARE

“To be an artist is to fail, as no other dare fail.” Samuel Beckett

End of the story. Or the beginning of the story.

We are all on different journeys, and we can only inspire others along the way. **Do what you can** in life to make this world a better place. And art is a great way to start.

In essence, all artists uproot themselves. That's why they stand out.

To survive, plant your roots in the clouds to always remain free, and in transition.

Artists
can
always
be reborn.

CURSE 365–A NEW LIFE

Artists die.

www.ingramcontent.com/pod-product-compliance
Lightning Source LLC
LaVergne TN
LVHW091401190726
843491LV00006B/1206

* 9 7 8 3 9 4 9 3 9 2 1 4 6 *